For my mother,

Ivey Cotton.

Thank you for all the years of carefully tilling my soil.

Her children rise up and call her blessed;
her husband also, and he praises her:
"Many women have done excellently,
but you surpass them all."

Proverbs 31:28-29, ESV

Special thanks to my brother, Jeff, for inspiring me to write all this down in the first place, to my husband, Steve, for letting me throw ashes on him and take pictures of it, and also to him and my children for indulging me the hours that went into writing, to Jessica and Beth for being sounding boards, to Maribeth for capturing the cover images, and to all of my family and friends who read bits and gave feedback over the last four years, and to Teague for doing the polishing work. I've never had a stranger help me so generously. Thanks also to biblehub.com for all of the fantastic free resources. May God bless each of you all richly!

# The Book of Job:

## Seeing God through the Ashes

# Chapter 1

## The Saga Begins

"Come to me, all you who are weary and burdened, and I will give you rest.  Take my yoke upon you and learn from me, for I am gentle and humble in heart, and you will find rest for your souls."  (Matt 11:28 & 29, NIV)

Life can be overwhelming when we find ourselves deep in the pit surrounded by darkness and fear.  It is often no easier to understand for those of us who have grown up believing that there is a God.  We were taught He loves and protects us, answers our prayers, and provides for our needs.  But He can seem like an imaginary dream when the reality of life hits us square in the face.  Where is God?  Why is this happening?  How do I get out of here?  When does it stop?  Why does everything seem to fall apart at once?

The pain of human struggle is obvious.  When it becomes personal, there is often a crisis of faith.  How can God be both loving and in control if tragedy is the norm?  Surely, if He loved me, then He would protect me from this.  If He is all powerful and can see all my pain, then why doesn't He stop it from happening?  It leaves us with feelings of fear and doubt.  Is everything we've been taught about God true?

Who is He?  What is He like?  If we know the truth about this, we can trust Him when all is dark.  If we are not rock solid on what His character is like, then we may distrust His motives and actions in the deafening silence.

To get to know His character we must pick up His Words and read them for ourselves. We must spend time in one-on-one conversation with Him, set aside our preconceived notions, and ask Him to show us who He is. A personal, trusting relationship with God doesn't depend on a church pew, a podcast, a feeling you get on a campout, or even a good Christian book. These are only tools. We must personally spend quality time with Him.

There comes a time in every Christian life to mature in our relationship with God. It is a time when we go from hearing what God is like from our mentors and teachers to knowing Him because we have seen Him for ourselves (Job 42:5-6). It takes a life-changing encounter with Him to turn our world right side up. For some of us, that encounter sounds like a whisper; for others, it comes in a whirlwind. For all of us, it takes a heart ready to listen.

This is the story we find written in the pages of Job. It is a saga told for generations of one man who went from hearing that Almighty God was a slave driver, beating mankind whenever we step out of line, arbitrarily giving and taking away according to His mysterious whim, to seeing Creator Yahweh as a merciful and compassionate God of relationship.

For some of us it will be the first time you've cracked your Bible on your own. For others, your Bible is well loved and worn. Either way, there is something there for everyone. Pick yours up. Look in the table of contents. You will find a book there. Its name is Job. It is full of profound answers on who God is and what to do with all this pain is in your life.

In order to get the most out of this human's look at Job, I encourage you to read the whole book of Job out of your

Bible first.  It will give us a starting point, common ground to begin discovering the meaning that we can apply to our own pain like salve to an open wound.  No really, go read it.  I will even mark your spot on the page so you can find it when you get back.  You can skim if you want to; we'll hash out God's answer a little later.  But you need the big picture in your head.  Otherwise, the things you read in this book will seem shocking—like the fact that Job questions God and wishes he was dead.  I suggest you find an easy-to-read version for this study, but if you love your old faithful version, feel free to stick with it.  It doesn't matter, just read it.  Or even easier, you can go to biblegateway.com and listen to it for free in almost any version you want.  Each chapter only takes two or three minutes, and you can be done in less than two hours.

~~~~~~~Paused for Reading Job~~~~~~~

When I reached my own crisis of faith, the Book of Job was the first place I turned.  I had heard rumors about a man who went through great tragedy and came out of it twice as great as he was before.  He was full of quotable one-liners like, "The Lord giveth, and the Lord taketh away."  I had the impression from Sunday school stories that he was the wisest, holiest man because he endured such trouble without a peep or a bad attitude.

Imagine my surprise when I read the whole book for myself!  My first reading left me with more questions than answers.  It seemed like God singled out His best player to His rival.  Satan asked if he could play a little sport with Job's life to see if he could get him to quit the game.  God enthusiastically agreed to the challenge.  A bunch of bad stuff happened to a perfectly good man.  Job's friends tried to convince him it was his own fault by saying things I heard in church regularly. Job got depressed and angry. Finally, God berated Job for four chapters because he didn't understand anything. As quickly as it started, the game was over. God restored all of Job's stuff. Everyone lived happily ever after. Clap your hands together. The End. What!? That's it? Where are all the answers? It seemed like all the important parts I was looking for were missing.

My first pass at Job was entirely frustrating. I found myself amening Job's friends' theology. I highlighted their words of "wisdom" until I got to the end and found they were all wrong and had to make amends for the way they lied about God's character. Even Job, who is the hero here, repented in dust and ashes for his prior beliefs about God (Job 42:6).

They said God was big and powerful; we are but wretched peons in His sight. He has the right to treat His creation anyway He sees fit. God spanks the bad people and blesses His good children. God has a predestined plan; our only duty is to fulfill it. The bad things we experience are God's punishment for our failure; we reap what we sow.

When this formula doesn't fit with reality or seems evil, the only answer given is that God is so far beyond human understanding that His plans are incomprehensible. Some things are just ordained, and we have to deal with it correctly in order to pass God's test. Repent of your secret unfaithfulness.

I have heard each of these "truths" preached. Even Job agreed with their theology. That's why he spends so much of the book confused as to why all this bad stuff was happening to him, angry at God for not upholding His end of the bargain. The formula he understood didn't work.

When I got to the end of the story, my frustration compounded. Why did God use a whole book of the Bible to describe His answers to the problem of evil so vaguely? I am in the pit here! I don't have enough energy to get up, let alone the spiritual capacity to see through all the poetry. Other than being rude, how were Job's friends wrong?

I found that, in my pain, I had hurriedly skimmed through the answer God provided. I was scrambling for meaning to what was going on in my life, searching for why this was happening to me. I wanted a quick, easily digested answer. In my haste, I missed the gentle truths laid out there.

The first time through, I felt even more jaded than when I picked up the book, but I kept on reading. I didn't want to give up on my childhood faith until I had read the whole Bible completely. I figured at least then I could say that I had done all that I could, and those who chose to stay in the faith couldn't use peer pressure or guilt to manipulate me into coming back to a dead, useless belief system. I would be able to defend my reasons for leaving. I was determined to have a fully satisfying relationship with God, or I was going to quit the whole church thing. Going through the motions of religion would just be a waste of my time and precious, little energy.

I found a clue to the true meaning of Job when I got to the opposite end of my Bible in the book of James. James 5:11 says, "We count those blessed who endured. You have heard of the endurance of Job and have seen the outcome of the Lord's dealings, that the Lord is full of compassion and is merciful" (NASB). What was God revealing through His dealings in the Book of Job? That the Lord is full of compassion and is merciful!

I've heard many sermons on Job the man, but I had never heard someone talk from the book of Job about the character of God—especially that He is compassionate and merciful!

The only messages I really remembered were lauding the super-hero endurance of a man who withstood all the bad stuff in his life and, even more importantly, didn't shame himself by blaming God. Is that really all we can take away from this book? As it turns out, that's not even true! Job ranted at God several times.

Needless to say, those sermons were not very helpful during my crisis. At best, they left me admiring the thought of doing the right thing but feeling completely inadequate to accomplish it. Those talks were just tips about what I needed to be doing to *act* like a servant of God. Their effect was actually detrimental to that cause because they did nothing to help me put my trust in God when I didn't understand what He was doing. I felt that if God wasn't going to protect me, I needed to protect myself. This made my behavior even less loving and Christ-like; I acted extremely selfishly instead.

By pointing out my failures of faith, those messages made me want to give up on the whole idea of Christianity. Being good was impossible and didn't produce the protection and provision that my heart longed for anyway. In my deep desolation, I knew I was not big enough to *do* enough. I could never measure up. I was on my own to find value, joy, and security. It was hopeless. If God didn't protect the most perfect man on earth, how was I to ever get what I needed? I didn't deserve it. I'm wretched! How can I do the right thing if that's not who I am? I'm just programmed to do wrong by both nature and nurture, and I can't fix it. Why would God love and care for me if I'm like that?

People talked about how trusting God gave them peace, but I didn't understand how that could be possible. I couldn't wrap my brain around trusting a God who let such horrible things happen.  He didn't seem trustworthy.  I also didn't understand how hoping in an invisible, silent God would give me peace of mind.  Trust didn't change the events of life; it was only a crutch to make it through them.  All the talk about trusting God because He had a plan was the antithesis of what I needed to hear in order to actually trust Him.  If God chooses to treat me like this, who needs Him?

Since I couldn't fix my problems and God seemingly chose not to, despair took over.  Is the Christian life only about gritting your teeth until this season of pain is over?  Am I only looking forward to the fact that someday "I'll Fly Away"?  Am I supposed to plaster a smile on my face and praise God on the outside if I am screaming in pain on the inside (Job 9:27-28)?

The short answer to all of these questions is no.  We don't have to grin and bear it, or fake it till we make it.  Expressing our frustration with our circumstances is not a sin; in fact, it may be one of the most important steps to authentically confronting our issues of faith.

More importantly, we can do more than just talk about change.  We can live powerfully, joyfully free right now, even in a turbulent reality.  All of this does not come from fixing our behavior; we can never do enough to deserve it.  It comes from being in a living relationship with God who loves us because that is His character, not based on what we've done to make Him like us.  This is fully available to every one of us through Jesus, not just a limited few.

Jesus told us the reason that he came to Earth, "I am come that they might have life, and that they might have it more abundantly" (John 10:10, KJV).  It is this verse that catapulted me into a frenzied search for answers.  It haunted me that the life I had was not all there was.  Life abundantly was the farthest description from what I was experiencing!  Hell on earth is more what it felt like. There was nothing in my circumstances that brought any spark of joy: not at home, not at work, not my health, not my relationships. Nothing. There was only the constant darkness threatening to swallow me whole.

The problem was that my joy fluctuated with my circumstances. I didn't have the tools to disconnect my peace of mind from the turbulence around me and place it on the character of God. At the time, it seemed to me like my circumstances were a reflection of how God felt about me; the two things were inextricably linked. This left me feeling as though God had abandoned me to my troubles. He must despise me. He had the power to fix it all, but He chose not to for some cruel reason. He planned my misery.

Jesus I could trust; God seemed totally random and obscure. Jesus obviously loved me. No one would voluntarily sacrifice Himself like that for anything less than a passionate love. I had fallen in love with Him as a little girl when He called the little children to Him as all the other "important" people shooed them away. Later in life when I felt worthless, it made me feel accepted to read He ate dinner with the outcasts of His time. I cheered Him on when He brought the religious leaders down a peg or two from their prideful place of judgment. But God in the Old Testament seemed foreboding and scary, like an angry authoritarian with His hand raised in constant threat; I couldn't see any unconditional love there.

The disparity came because I had only heard about God in the Old Testament from selected stories. I had never read the whole thing for myself. I had never seen Him. Jesus said, "He who has seen Me has seen the Father" (John 14:9, NASB). How could Jesus be the full picture of who God is if they seemed so different? The Trinity seemed more like three distinct, schizophrenic, unrelated parts rather than one, unified entity. It was utterly confusing.

With James 5 in mind, I took who Jesus said God is and re-read the Book of Job again. And there I saw Him, a loving Father waiting for me with open arms, ready to set me free from all fear, from all the chains I was wearing as a religious slave. He was ready for me to be His mature child and full heir to His Kingdom. There was so much I had missed when I read the story focused on Job and focused on finding a quick answer to my own pain.

The result of this new reading was that I felt like the older son in the parable of the prodigal, but with a different ending (Luke 15:11-31). Instead of being bitter at having obeyed all this time with nothing to show for it, I wanted to throw my arms around the Father and tell Him I was sorry for misrepresenting Him. Now, with my whole heart, I want to make His vision my vision, His passion my passion, His love my love. I want to find every hurting prodigal and tell them what valuable treasure they are. I want to hug all those rule-followers like me and say stop trying so hard to be worthy; just be loved and express love in return. Forget the measuring line. The Father loves us all. Now we can truly live a life of love.

Since I can't literally put my arms around your neck and tell you how much you are loved, I am writing this book to you to explain how a trusting relationship with God pulled me out of my black hole and brought me into a life of hope and confidence. Prodigal brother, obedient brother, or otherwise, God is watching for us like the good father in the story, waiting with arms open wide to have a loving relationship!

What would it have looked like if the prodigal's older brother had opened his heart and gone from obeying because it was his duty and he wanted something from his father, to obeying because it was his passion to love his father? It would look exactly like the book of Job.

The changes are subtle. Yet things are said redundantly so that we can finally see the comparison of who Job was at the end of the book with who he was at the beginning. In both places he is diligent and obedient. He is careful and contrite. He wants to do the right thing. He completely believes God and acts on those beliefs.

Yet at the beginning of Job we see a man working for approval from God, frantically making sacrifices just in case his kids *might* have sinned (Job 1:5). We see a man who believes we reap what we sow; therefore, he is determined only to sow good things in his life. You could say he was obsessive compulsive about it. He had a need to control the details in an attempt to control the outcomes, obedience in exchange for provision and protection. His dedication was admirable, but the type of fear which motivated him was unhealthy for the human condition. It was more like slavery than a true relationship with God.

At the end of Job we find a man who is happy, generous and satisfied, interceding for others on God's behalf. He had a true, trusting relationship with God and a better relationship with people. Love overflowed into his actions, not because he made a covenant with himself to do the right thing, but because he learned that he was loved and cared for without having to earn it. He loved and cared for others without regard to status or worthiness. His life was full and fulfilling. I can't wait to get to that part! It makes me want to race ahead, so that we can sit together and feast on the joy found in parsing out the details of the last few paragraphs. I'm excited to revel with you in the pure joy of loving a God who absolutely, unconditionally loves us first.

Job's story *does* hold all of the profound answers I was looking for but missed the first time through. They are thinly veiled in allegory and metaphor. It does not give pat answers to messy problems but does show us how and why we can trust the character of God even in the darkest moments. Job is all about the fact "that the Lord is full of compassion and is merciful."

This answer changed me much more than the ones I was expecting to find there. I was looking for: Why me, why this, why now, why not them, what am I supposed to do now? All of my questions were "me" focused. The right questions to ask the book of Job are God focused. Who is God, and why should I trust Him in the midst of all this craziness? If we can figure that out, then the "me" questions will find answers too. It does not work well the other way around. If we start with "me" focused questions, we will miss the point of Job and end up with answers skewed toward our predispositions and prejudices.

The book of Job has four chapters of God Himself explaining that He is compassionate and merciful. It tears down our misconceptions about God and His motives, and then it builds a new understanding of the character of God, concept upon concept.

It uses beautiful literary tools to accomplish this. The book of Job is a timeless work of sacred art that paints a picture of God with His creation. Though it's difficult to see in our English versions, the book was originally written partly in prose and partly in poetry. I believe this is because it is a true story used to make a much grander point; the facts of Job's story are written in prose, and then the imagery of poetry is used to explain the truth. Poetry allows the reader to engage with the story across cultures and eras. It allows us access to the truth layer by layer as we dig for understanding, rather than assaulting us with more than our little minds can take in at once. This is both for our protection and to engender relationship rather than rote memorization of the facts. God wants us to know Him, but allows us to find Him by choice at our own pace rather than forcing Himself on us. Sure, it might be easier to have everything black and white, but poetry encodes far more information into the limited space offered by a hand written, vellum scroll.

As poetry, the book of Job uses superlatives to cast a wide net so that its target audience includes everyone who reads it. For example, Job is the greatest man in the East. I believe that God chose to describe Job as the "greatest" so that no matter where we fall in the spectrum of society, we could not claim to be better than Job. He was the richest, most powerful, most religious man in the land, described by God Himself as blameless and upright. Can any of us claim that? Even as a strict rule follower, I cannot assert that I am totally blameless. Can you? Job, as a portrayal of human perfection, represents the extreme outer limits of what can be accomplished by our own planning and efforts. His good deeds were greater than what any of us could ever hope to do. We cannot earn more rewards or protect ourselves from pain any better than Job did. What happened to him could happen to all of us.

As high as Job set the bar for perfection in order to include us in the story, he also went to the deepest depths of despair to include us in the story. We cannot feel more betrayed by God than Job. His story is a type of worst case scenario. He lost everything at once—his health, wealth, family, status, power, respect, and anything else you could think of—in one day. Stripped of all but dust and ashes, he was suicidal, wishing he were dead, yet unable to break the rule and murder himself. Instead, he asked God to finish the job and do it for him. No matter how depressed and fearful we are,

Job, the most humanly righteous man that ever existed, was right there too. Belief in the existence of God doesn't protect us from experiencing fear. In fact, depending on our beliefs about the nature of God, our fear may be worse than if we didn't believe at all.

The Book of Job is for everyone, the highest of the high to the lowest of the low. No matter what our starting point, it is meant to bring us into a relationship with a God who is merciful and full of compassion. Rather than giving one-size-fits-all answers to the complicated questions of "why me" and "why this," it reveals the character of a trustworthy God. Nothing will allay our fears like trust in a God who loves us all without limits, who is actively working to make us the best that we can be.

Before we move on to see how this is possible, now would be a great time to take a few minutes to ask God to reveal Himself to you. Pray and ask Him what He is really like. It doesn't have to be some fancy, flowery composition. Just lay it all out there, give Him your pain, and put all of your questions on the table. He can handle the fact that you are doubting and mistrusting. Don't try to hide anything. Open communication is one of the key foundations to a good relationship. Building a real relationship with God on the inside is far more important at this stage than outwardly being proper or following the rules people have told us. Respect for God is vital to a thriving relationship, but you won't ever truly have it if you don't address what is keeping you from actually believing He is respectable. Start with an honest prayer.

If you are struggling with depression on any level, add to that prayer one for guidance on any steps you should take in the physical realm. He may lead you to get your hormones checked, change your diet, exercise, get your blood work done, quit an addiction, see a therapist, an allergist, an acupuncturist, or a nutritionist, etc. It may be different for you, but for me, it is hard to change anything spiritual if I'm ignoring when my body is screaming at me to pay attention. There is no spiritual shame in getting physical help along the way. Life change is a holistic experience, not just a philosophical endeavor. Go all in and make changes as you become aware of them. As someone who has been there, it will make a huge difference in the ease of your journey.

Knowing God more intimately has not suddenly made life all cherries and roses, but my pain has been turned into empowerment, and even when life turns upside-down again, I have peace beyond explanation. I no longer live in constant, hopeless depression and misery; rather I have confidence and joy. I am not unique; this is available for everyone. That's because it has nothing to do with me or my constitution as a person; it has everything to do with who God is and His intentions toward humanity, all of humanity. That means that you too can live a life of joy and peace even in this crazy, messed-up world. Don't give up; let's go on an expedition through the book of Job together to find the answers.

No matter if you are beginning this journey as religious slave like Job, in the prodigal's pig sty, or, like me, somewhere wavering between the two, my desire is that by the end of this book you will have a whole new outlook on your value, hope, and security. I pray that through the Almighty's answer you will find a God who is compassionate and merciful, a Father you can trust with all you are. My hope is that you will be able to live a life free from fear, full of confidence, joy, and empowerment. May you find life abundantly!

## Chapter 2

## A Day in Court

"Be sober, be vigilant; because your adversary the devil, as a roaring lion, walketh about, seeking whom he may devour:" (1 Pet 5:8, KJV)

The first issue that plagued me when I read the Book of Job for myself was the interaction between God and Satan. Chapters one and two seemed to portray God as a cosmic bully using His great power to sic the devil on His most loyal servant. Is that really what happened? Let's take a deeper look.

> One day the angels came to present themselves before the Lord, and Satan also came with them.
>
> The Lord said to Satan, "Where have you come from?"
>
> Satan answered the Lord, "From roaming throughout the earth, going back and forth on it."
>
> Then the Lord said to Satan, "Have you considered my servant Job? There is no one on earth like him; he is blameless and upright, a man who fears God and shuns evil."
>
> "Does Job fear God for nothing?" Satan replied. "Have you not put a hedge around him and his household

and everything he has? You have blessed the work of his hands, so that his flocks and herds are spread throughout the land. But now stretch out your hand and strike everything he has, and he will surely curse you to your face."

The Lord said to Satan, "Very well, then, everything he has is in your power, but on the man himself do not lay a finger."

Then Satan went out from the presence of the Lord. (Job 1:6-12, NIV)

There is a lot of information in this short interaction for us to understand. The simplest point to make is that Satan exists. He is real, not just a fairy-tale boogeyman. He should not be given too much power in our theology, but neither should his role be ignored. He is our accuser in the court of heaven. His very name means "adversary, accuser, or slanderer." As our accuser, his intents and actions have a huge effect on what is happening in our lives.

A great portion of Job's frustration and confusion stemmed from the fact that he didn't seem to take Satan into the equation at all. He had not witnessed the scene in heaven prior to all of his troubles. He didn't see Satan come before God or hear the accusation against him. He did not see Satan go out from God's presence intent on tearing him to shreds. He did not understand how or why anything was happening. Job attributed every ounce of his pain directly to the hand of God alone.

Observers assessing Job's situation today might say he was unlucky, or they might assume it was just a random string of events with no connection to the spiritual world. Yet the Bible gives us glimpses of an enemy who is trying to crush us.

1 Peter 5:8 also illustrates how Satan is working. He is hunting humanity like a lion, prowling for an opportunity to swallow us up. This is the exact description given to us at the beginning of Job's story. He had just come from "roaming throughout the earth, going back and forth on it" (Job 1:7, 2:2, NIV). Satan stalked about Job looking for just the right attack.

He needed a good plan. He wanted to destroy Job, but Job had a hedge of protection around him. There was no getting to the man without permission from God himself. Once he found a reason for God to let him touch Job, he had to humble himself and ask.

What better day to do that than on a day formally set aside for angels to present themselves before God to receive their next assignment. Satan showed up in heaven on just such a day. His presence there would have been suspicious from the start since Satan makes a point of *not* taking orders from God, of *not* following his assignments. It would be like a baseball player who quit the team showing up on game day wearing his old uniform and wondering what base he was going to play. No wonder God responded with, "Where'd you come from?"

Since the angels were there to report and to receive assignments, Satan had an opportunity to take advantage of the system. The right orders might suit his purpose. He wanted the legal right to be granted the cudgel of punishment (Is. 10:5). With it, he could beat Job senseless. He could consume his prey, and God would not intervene on Job's behalf.

There's a lot of passion stewing just below the surface that English just does not portray for us. This part of the conversation between God and Satan is like a father asking his child covered in mud what he's been doing. As a parent he knew before he ever asked that the little trouble-maker had been hopping puddles in his church clothes. It's an offence worthy of using his middle name. Yet most kids still try to deny or defend their infraction despite the obvious.

In the same way, Satan dodged God's inquiry. Eventually God told Satan what he already knew about his actions and motives. God knew exactly where Satan had been, what he had been doing, and why.

Modern readers may better relate to the scene in heaven if it read more like this:

> Now, on the day when the sons of God (aka angels) take their stations according to the Lord's assignments, Satan slipped in among their ranks.
>
> "Satan, where have you been?" asked Yahweh. (Though Satan was originally created as one of the angels, it had been years since Satan had left heaven in a fit of rebellion. His voluntary presence now was highly suspicious.)
>
> "Oh, nowhere, just taking a stroll around the earth." Satan replied in his most innocent voice, as if treading down the earth was his last assignment rather than an act of defiance.
>
> Aware of Satan's intent, God cut to the chase, "You saw my most upright, perfect servant Job while you were there. I know you're interested in him because there is no one like him on the face of the earth. He is blameless and fears me instead of you. He refuses to give in to your temptations, and you can't stand it. You've set your heart on him, haven't you?"

That tricky phrase, "Have you considered my servant Job?" isn't at all what I first imagined. God isn't asking Satan as if He did not already know the answer. The three Hebrew words interpreted "considered" or "noticed" in most versions of the Bible are literally "set heart on." God did not point at Job and say, "Hey, have you noticed how wonderful my servant Job is? Have you ever considered what he might do if we mess with him?" Not at all! God was telling Satan He knew what Satan was up to: stalking God's most righteous servant. God knew Satan had "set his heart on" Job. Maybe it's a reflection of modern society that when we read the word "considered," we take it lightly as in a moment of passing thought like choosing the best option at a fast food joint, rather than the intended description of Satan's obsessive, infatuated brooding over Job.

However, Satan is not a small child with mud on his pants ready to blurt out his guilt. It wasn't his first go around with breaking the law of love and trying to get away with it. He had a strategy for bypassing all those introspective questions. He diverted attention from his own motives and directed them back to Job.

Through all his obsession and pacing, studying Job and digging into his personal life, Satan could find nothing to accuse in Job's actions. As God said, Job was blameless. He followed every rule and even made up a few extra. Job 1 tells us he made sacrifices on behalf of his children "just in case" they had broken a rule. He was OCD about following every rule. There was only one technicality that Satan could find in Job's hedge of protection. It wasn't a behavioral issue; it was a heart issue. The only thing the Accuser could use to prosecute Job was his motivation.

> "Yes, but Job only obeys you because of what you do for him by blessing him with stuff. You've built up a wall of protection around him, but he doesn't love you the way you want or deserve. How can you say he is one of yours, a member of the kingdom of love? He only

does what you want because he's scared. It's not because he loves you or anyone else. He's just using you. Though his actions look like love, he is as selfish as any man. Therefore, he is one of mine! Now, cut him off from your kingdom! Erase his name from your holy roster of life."

God's answer is astonishing. It's not at all what I would have expected. Rather than defending Job because of all of his good deeds, He says, "Behold, all that he has is in your power, only do not put forth your hand on him" (NASB). This word "Behold" is unfamiliar to most of us these days. In other places in the Bible it is interpreted "see, indeed, surely." The NIV interprets it, "very well." It is a positive affirmation. God in this one little word says, "Indeed, I see." In other words, "Yes, I know." Job obeys God perfectly, but in a do-to-get manner, not out of faith, trust, or love.

Since true obedience to God has always been about a relationship and expressing love out of a grateful heart, simple rule following for self-preservation was not enough to protect Job from Satan's accusation. Though technically a Law follower, Job was guilty of selfishness. All Job's good works were for himself. God affirms he was motivated by rewards for his good actions and fear of being punished for any bad actions. That is why he followed the rules as perfectly as any man could. Job's reward-and-punishment theology was focused entirely on the principle we often call sowing and reaping. This type of religion is excruciating!

A self-centered worldview whether religious or irreligious leaves us captive to fear, pride, and self-deprecation which leads to more fear and pain. God could not let His beloved Job live a life captive to fear. He is determined for us all to live a life of freedom and authority based on a relationship with the Creator. The entire theme of the book is to open

Job's eyes to the fact that God is not just a hall monitor watching us from way up in the sky enforcing the rules with lightning bolts and hailstones, or even with ponies and good-boy stickers; God is a God of love and compassion. To free Job from his fear of punishment and his false sense of legalistic pride, God set in motion the circumstances that Job needed in order to question his religious presuppositions.

(Keep your eye on this theme. The whole Book of Job is about breaking down belief in a controlling god whose sole purpose is dispensing justice, and replacing that theology with a God who is compassionate and merciful.)

Rather than directly stretching out His hand to strike Job's world as Satan provoked Him to do, God relinquished authority over Job and his possessions to Satan.

The authority God gave Satan came with certain parameters. The limits to Satan's authority were directly correlated to everything Job was trusting in for value, happiness, and security. Satan was allowed to remove the blessings Job thought he'd earned with his obedience.

Satan left the courtroom bent on destruction. Job would fear him now! (Job 3:25) His authority over Job was temporary and limited, but he'd push the limits of the sentence as far as he could get away with. His intention was to show this peon human he was garbage and get him to curse God, making him a permanent member of the Kingdom of Hell. He wanted to hold Job captive in fear and hopelessness. He needed to destroy Job's faith in the Creator and rip him apart while the whole world watched. He'd spin the story far and wide. He'd use Job like a corner pin to knock down as many other people as he could. Let the human race see that Job's way of life was useless; following God has no reward. God does not love or protect even His most faithful of servants.

Don't bother with obedience. Satan obliterated Job's whole world in one day.

At first, Job seemed to take it on the chin. What was Job's reaction? Worship. *Worship*?! That was definitely not my first response. "The Lord gave and the Lord has taken away; may the name of the Lord be praised" (Job 1:21b). It sounds like Job was quoting a hymn he'd learned as a boy. (But notice it was not the Lord who had taken away, rather Satan had destroyed.)

When taking all that Job feared losing didn't cause Job to abandon God completely and permanently, Satan went back to God with a new charge (Job 2:1-7). I can almost see Satan foaming at the mouth with hatred and venom as he spat out his accusations—frustrated and angry. "Skin for skin! Yes, all that a man has he will give for his life" (NIV). In other words, "Any man will save his own backside by offering the hide of some else. Job didn't curse you because he has not suffered personally. Someone else suffered. He didn't die, only his children and servants. No man cares about what happens to other people as long as the pain isn't personal." It is almost as if Satan is not only accusing Job, but all mankind of loving themselves more than anyone else—even their own children. In truth, it is often an accurate accusation (read 2 Kgs 20:16-19 for just one example).

Satan incited God to destroy Job right then and there for such evil. Forget waiting until the final judgment, Job was already convicted of living on the dark side.

There must have been a shade of truth to the accusation, because once again God admitted Satan's authority over Job and this time allowed him to lay his hands on Job's body. Satan was permitted to be as personal as possible without taking his life. "So Satan went out from the presence of the Lord and [Satan] afflicted Job..." (Job 2:7a, NIV). He literally went after Job's skin as if it was a manifestation of his accusation.

God did not call down lightning bolts from heaven to strike Job as Job had assumed He would. Instead, Satan, obsessed with an upright man, attacked with all the vehemence that God would allow.

This is the last glimpse behind the scenes we get. From here on out we have to stumble through the story with Job. We have to try to figure out what is going on right along with our main character. We get to feel his frustration as he asks the familiar questions brought on by pain and suffering. This behind the scenes drama allows us to see that the turmoil of life is not simply God punishing us for mistakes. It is so much more than that. It is not just linear action between us and God. In this instance, at least, there is a court room with rules of order and procedure.

Our enemy is not the Judge; it is the Prosecutor. The Judge dispenses justice without prejudice. His intent is to bring about repentance and rehabilitation, not merely revenge or punishment. He provides the perfect circumstances to empower us to change, to bring freedom from the way of thinking that has held us captive to fear and self destruction. In stark contrast, the Prosecutor just wants to annihilate humans or at a minimum lock us up for good, leaving nothing left of us to fight him.

In his arrogance, Satan thought he'd won this round. Yet God takes all of Satan's destructive exertion and turns it back on him. By the end of the story Job isn't just doing the right thing. He is free from fear, and he has a fulfilling relationship with God.

# Chapter 3

## Sovereign Love

"For the LORD is a great God, and a great King above all gods." (Ps 95:3, ESV)

The second thing that troubled me about the Book of Job was that the friend's theology was what I had grown up hearing at church and at school. Yet, in the end God was angry with them because they had not spoken the truth about His character. The men of the East, including Job, all believed that God is great and sovereign. Every word they spoke and every choice they made was to honor the fact that God was high and holy. It is true that God is perfect and sovereign; there are hundreds of verses we could quote to prove it, so what is the problem with their belief system?

A good summery of their beliefs is found in chapter four. Job's great-uncle Eliphaz tried to comfort Job by encouraging him to be pious, then he ended the speech like this:

> Dread came upon me, and trembling, And made all my bones shake. Then a spirit passed by my face; The hair of my flesh bristled up. It stood still, but I could not discern its appearance; A form was before my eyes; There was silence, then I heard a voice:

"Can mankind be just before God? Can a man be pure before his Maker? He puts no trust even in His servants; And against His angels He charges error. How much more those who dwell in houses of clay, Whose foundation is in the dust, Who are crushed before the moth! Between morning and evening they are broken in pieces; Unobserved, they perish forever. Is not their tent-cord plucked up within them? They die, yet without wisdom." (Job 4:14-21, NASB)

It all sounds very reasonable. In fact, just last summer I heard a man standing on a lamp post screaming this very message at passersby during a walk in the park with my family. I've seen men and women with picket signs on TV bellowing it at funeral caravans. It's what the secular world thinks religion is all about; God says people are bad and need to be punished.

Yet, if it's completely true, then why do we hear it coming out of the mouth of a scary demon in the night? Never trust the whispers of your nightmares to tell you the *whole* truth. The source should send up red flags!

Problem number one with this theology is that it keeps us permanently separated from God. We can never have a relationship with the Almighty for the same reason a moth cannot have a relationship with a gardener. He is high and magnificent, and we are low and miniscule. The two are incompatible.

The night terror implied that because God is so far above us, He would never stoop down to soil Himself with our problems. He won't even lean one level down and dirty His hands with the angels, let alone go all the way to the bottom of the totem pole where humanity wallows in the mire. Snuffing us out would be as easy and thoughtless for Him as it would be for us to crush a moth. Once we fail, we're abandoned to our fate. There is no hope of finding life abundantly. Humanity is destined to wander through life like nomads only to die without wisdom. Our very beginnings foreshadow our end, ashes to ashes, dust to dust.

The patriarchs from the East agreed wholeheartedly with the demonic message. They believed in the greatness of God, but not His goodness. They thought His greatness meant He micro-managed every detail of life on earth and heaven. As you read the rest of the speeches between Job and his friends, the vast supremacy of God and the wretchedness of man are the main point. In their minds, justice was the ultimate rule in the universe. This even led Job's friends to condemn him because his suffering must have been nothing less than God's justice against a wicked man.

When we believe God is only a far off entity with no desire for relationship, the only means we have for a happy life is to work the system to the best of our ability. We can choose the secular system and toss God completely aside to milk this world for all it has to offer. Or, we can choose to play the religious game and dance the fine line between obeying the rules enough to get what we want and finding an easy road to happiness. Either way we will lose out on the one thing that will actually fill our hearts to the full: unconditional love and honor.

The religion of the East was saturated with the belief that God is too great to care about stupid, little humans. It wasn't just a phantom in the night preaching such things. All of Job's friends reiterated it at one point or another. For instance Bildad said:

> "Dominion and awe belong to God; he establishes order in the heights of heaven. Can his forces be numbered? On whom does his light not rise? How then can a mortal be righteous before God? How can one

born of woman be pure? If even the moon is not bright and the stars are not pure in his eyes, how much less a mortal, who is but a maggot—a human being, who is only a worm!" (Job 25:1-6, NIV)

Their theology pushed God into a far off distance. He is unknowable and beyond us. In comparison humans are thought of as garbage, worth less than dirt. This is only a partial truth.

We are *not* as awesome as God. He is vast and incomparable! It is important for us to realize we are not God, and His ways are greater than ours.

The other side of the story is that God created humanity to govern the earth (Gen 1:26-28, 2 Tim 2:11-13, Rev 22:1-5). He made us in His own image as if we were His very own children (Gen 5:1, Luke 3:38). He then died for us while we were still rejecting Him (Rom 5:6-8). We are not maggots to Him! We cannot hold our head up high and say we are god, but God is the "lifter of my head" (Ps 3:3). He paid full price for broken goods because we are treasure to Him even in our brokenness. Whenever we feel like maggots—especially because we have failed—that is our own humanistic point of view, never God's (Ps 8:4-9).

It is just as prideful to say that humans are wretched worms because of what we have done as it is to say we are like God. Either way our worth is still based on us, our rank, and what we do or don't do. It is not humility to have low self-esteem. Humility is taking the word "self" out of esteem. Our value is not based on how great or small we think we are. It is not related to how good we are. Instead, our worth is based on how much God was willing to pay to ransom us back from the Enemy. He gave up everything for us (Phil 2)! That is how much we are worth. We are made in the very image of God—His self-portrait!

Our vast, unmerited worth seems incomprehensible to the humanistic way of thinking. That is why God is incrementally revealing to Job God's way of thinking about the value of each member of His creation: We are worth dying for; we are worth blessing without merit.

The emphasis on God's holy greatness is only a half truth. As James 5:11 says the Book of Job is specifically written to reveal the mercy and compassion of our Creator. God is great, but the contrary is not true. We are not simply worthless dirt in His eyes. We will never go unnoticed and unloved no matter what we've done. God's justice and mercy are perfectly balanced on His love. There is not one without the other because God is love (1 John 4). Even in our brokenness, God honors us enough to gently humble Himself. He is seeking a relationship with lowly folks like us (Matt 11:28-30, Rom 5:1-11, Phil 2). He wants to rescue us from the muck and the mire of life (Ps 40:2).

God's love is what sets him apart from all other gods. Every god claims to be great. Their followers often shout it waving guns in the air. Only Yahweh says that the ultimate greatness is found in self-sacrificial love even for one's enemies (Phil 2:9). He is the only God I've ever studied who claims His kindness, mercy, patience, gentleness, and humility are the primary reasons we should follow Him and submit to His teachings (Matt 11:28-29, Rom 2:4). He seeks our trust, not just our obedience.

Understanding our inherent value in the eyes of God is pivotal to finding freedom and life abundantly. That's where the "endurance" description of Job becomes an important character quality (Jas 5:11). He didn't give up just because he found himself trapped by lies. When the truth he'd always known crashed head on into reality, he kept questioning his belief system until he found the truth. In the end, he found answers and freedom. Lies could no longer hold him captive. We need to stop listening to Satan's lies about God and us.

The very things God wants for us, Satan tells us are impossible. Relationship, value, and wisdom are all turned upside by his lies. Trust, the key relationship word, is spoken of as something so ludicrous that we must be morons to let it enter our minds. Satan takes the evidence of how the world works and interprets it for us the way he wants us to believe it. God takes the same set of evidence and reinterprets the data to reveal the truth: God loves even the worst offender.

Job had no idea that God loved him. Job was a religious slave bound by the law of sowing and reaping. He lived in fear of God's wrath. Job felt like he was walking on egg shells with God. Any wrong move and he might get zapped. He used the rules as a formula to get what he wanted out of life. He obeyed in order to receive provision and protection from an angry God.

This leads us to the second major issue with the friends' theology; it does nothing to change our heart. The religious system is based on fear of punishment and hope of reward. These can only affect our outward actions but do not produce love for our Maker. They offer no hope of a relationship with Him. This was the one thing Job was lacking. He technically followed the rules but did not live a life of love and kindness. In fact, if you read carefully, you'll see he was quite judgmental and harsh spoken. Since he thought God ruled by power and control, with anger and swift condemnation, Job spoke the same way to his wife about her words, to his friends, and about his employees.

His actions were a reflection of his beliefs about the nature of God. He thought God's kindness was a trick, an illusion. In chapter 10 he said, "You gave me life and showed me kindness, and in your providence watched over my spirit. But this is what you concealed in your heart, and I know that this was in your mind: If I sinned, you would be watching me and would not let my offense go unpunished" (NIV). While God can be kind, if you offend Him in any way, He's just waiting for the opportunity to destroy you (see Job 12). Job believed God has the ability to provide but the will to discipline.

This type of fear is not a balanced, healthy reverence for the true God. It's the immature fear of an untrusting child working for God to smile on him. This is the definition of a religious man. It is called legalism.

Without the love of God, we are left looking for ways to produce honor and safety for ourselves. The thing is, honor and safety describe what is happening on the outside of a person. Honor is given to those with status, and safety surrounds us like a protective cushion. Neither one has anything to do with what is happening inside our heart. It has nothing to do with love, joy, or peace. We can live in a bubble of honor and safety and still feel worthless, depressed, and fearful.

Satan tries to trick us into thinking the abundant life is freedom on the outside; it is the ability to go anywhere and do anything we want. To have this type of "freedom" we need status, power, and currency as tools to get the world to bend around us. We need control and authority. In this world's system things like worth, happiness, and peace are not inherent. Therefore, we must obsess over collecting them.

However, this focus on the outside usually leads to a life of captivity and fear on the inside. No matter how much we collect, it is never enough, and there is always someone with more. We must always be trying to prove we are bigger, better, smarter, and stronger. Fear of losing it all is always lurking in the shadows.

If power and currency are always out of reach, happiness may seem like a dark dream. A new job, a new relationship, or a new toy seem like just the thing to create happiness—until they are attained. When they fail, it is on to something new to create feelings of love, joy, and peace.

This may seem like a "them" problem if you enjoy the simple life. However, many of us do the same thing from our church pews today. If we cannot trust in the goodness of God, then love, joy, and peace still dwell outside of us and must be obtained. The motive of our heart remains the same as any secular man; we need worth, happiness, and a sense of security.

We are willing to use God as a means to acquire what we need, but we fail to engage in the relationship He offers us. Obedience and worship are simply currency to get what we want from God rather than being expressions of love and devotion. It is a do-to-get system. Our only power is gained by pushing others down or by manipulating God to get what we want. The result of this religion without relationship is either self-righteousness judgment or a continual cycle of selfishness and guilt. It can never produce our heart's desire.

When religion is the extent of our relationship to the Creator, we are left in fear that we haven't done enough to earn His good graces. We constantly worry whether or not our line in the sand is strict enough. The only way we can tell how we're doing is to compare ourselves with others. Regardless of whether we judge ourselves correctly, our attention is focused on our actions and acquisitions, not on developing a bond with our Maker.

If God will not look out for our best interest, there is no choice but for us to do it ourselves. Job did this very thing. He just did it in a religious way. He may not have set up idols or sacrificed to false gods to procure satisfaction for his soul's deepest needs, but his trust in wealth and power for his self-worth is dramatically evident by what he lamented losing. The riches he had accumulated as a result of obedience offered him a way to have honor and safety in this world. The loss of that honor and safety was the final blow which sent him plummeting into despair (Job 30:15-16).

Job thought his worth was dependant on his success just like the demon implied. It wasn't that the evidence was wrong. It wasn't that the Word of God was wrong. It was simply that he and his friends had listened to Satan's interpretation of the facts.

Some of the things the demon used as evidence were quite true. Sowing and reaping is a Law of the universe created by God (Gal 6:7-8). It's a fact that we have all failed to be as holy as God. It's true that we deserve to be punished. We will be judged at some point. It's reality that we're made out of dirt and will return to it.

However, the tenor of the statement was wrapped up in disparaging, belittling tones. It was a lie that humanity's worth to God is dependent on our level of perfection; humans are never just dirt to Him. God does not simply blow our dusty remains into oblivion because we failed, nor does He just pick the pretty ones that catch His fancy and throw the rest away.

God had a lot of work to do to change Job's long held beliefs. God is great and mighty, but that isn't all we need to believe. The fear of the Lord is only the beginning of wisdom, not the total sum of it. By the end of the book, Job repented in dust and ashes for believing God was far off and vengeful. Job became a whole new man.

At the beginning of the book, Job had status, power and wealth. He was working furiously to keep himself and his children safe from any possible harm. He followed the Law perfectly and even took extra precautionary measures just to make sure no one he loved could be found guilty. Yet he was half the man God intended for him to be. Compared to the end of the story, Job had half the stuff, half the children, half the employees, and half the relationship with God that God desired for him to have. He was the greatest man in the East, but he was still only half the man he could be, and he was afraid of losing it all. By the end of the story he went from being a rich authoritarian to being a generous intercessor on behalf of his people. He became fearless, full, and free.

I grew up with the idea that because he was "blameless," Job could not be wrong and everything he said was true. Yet as we saw in the last chapter, Job was blameless in his actions according to the Law, not necessarily in the motives of his heart. He obeyed out of duty, not love.

We all have great respect for Job as a righteous man who went through a lot. And we should! Seeing him as a human with flaws may feel unsettling. I don't know anyone alive today who would claim to be as righteous as Job, but he was just that—a human, a complex, multidimensional man, not just a storybook caricature of one. He had the same hurts and heartaches, frustrations and questions as the rest of us. There is much more to him than just a rich, goody two-shoes who stuck it out through the worst pain imaginable. The lessons we can learn from him go far beyond perseverance in trials; his story can lead us to trust the character of God.

You may be happy with the way things are right now, content with your status quo, but are you only half of what you could be? Are you afraid that what you have will be taken away? Would you be willing to go through what it takes to change your thinking in order to come out on the other side twice the person you are right now? Would you give up being an emotional millionaire to become a billionaire? I'm not talking about net-worth. That's irrelevant to a truly abundant life. I'm talking about self-worth. Would you be willing to give up your fear for peace and confidence? Would you be willing to give up your burdensome religion for a deep, satisfying relationship with God? This is what Job went through. The verdict Satan used to try to crush Job, God intended to use to set him free (Gen 50:20).

We are told in 2 Corinthians that "[God's] grace is sufficient for you, for power is perfected in weakness." It is often in our times of weakness that we finally allow the mold of what we have always thought, the way we have always done things, the way it has always been, to change. Change often seems too hard or scary. If it were left up to us, we would stay in our familiar captivity because it seems less stressful than change. It seems more plausible than what we do not understand.

Paul describes the peace of God as something "which transcends all understanding" (Phil 4:7). It is literally impossible to understand such peace until you've felt it. Once you've felt it, there's nothing else that even comes close to satisfying. You cannot know peace until you know the Prince of Peace. It is by trusting His character that we can let go of the bubble we're trying to maintain and finally live life abundantly free. Job's crisis was just the first step to achieving this lasting peace, but he had to endure to the end to find the answers provided by the Great I AM.

In reality, a God in heaven judging our deeds is only one small piece of the message God speaks to humanity about our relationship with Him. It is only a beginning step in understanding ourselves in comparison with God, but it is not intended to be the last step on our journey across the chasm created by sin. God's goodness is just as important to comprehend as His greatness.

In order to be truly holy as God intended, we need the one thing the demon in the night said we cannot hope for: the unconditional love of our Father God. His love changes us from the inside out, healing wounds and inspiring kindness. Without His love we are permanently separated from God unable to fulfill the Law we expect to save us.

Chapter 4

The Answers Begin

"Then the Lord answered Job out of the whirlwind and said:
"Who is this that darkens counsel by words without
knowledge?  Dress for action like a man; I will question you,
and you make it known to me" (Job 38:1-3, ESV).

God spoke to Job from a whirlwind with all of his friends
listening in.  Knowing what was missing in their faith, He went
about building a case for His unconditional love.

It takes an enormous amount of contrary evidence before
we'll reexamine our belief system.  Our belief system, whether
theistic or atheistic, is the filter by which we make decisions.  It
affects our identity and worth, our power and purpose, our
rationality and mental health.  To simply exchange it for
something new is nearly impossible; it takes unraveling a
person at the core and reweaving a whole new identity.  This
is far too demanding for most people to deal with outside of
a life altering crisis.  The longer we've been using our system of
beliefs, the more difficult it is to change.  The higher our beliefs
have brought us, the lower we have to go before letting go
of them.

This is exactly where we find Job when God steps into the
scene.  He has gone from the greatest man in the East to
being spat upon by those he believed unworthy to sleep with

his dogs.  His identity used to be "blameless law-keeper," but his belief in a God of justice who rewards the good and punishes the bad has been rocked to the core.  Who was he now that the foundation of his identity was gone?  The belief system he based everything on was disintegrated.

God's opening statements prepare Job for the major undertaking ahead:

> Who is this that obscures my plans with words without knowledge?  Brace yourself like a man; I will question you, and you shall answer me.  (Job 38:2-3, NIV)

Job and his friends had assumed a lot about God's plans.  Mostly it entailed punishment and pain.  Job needed to brace himself because he was about to go on a wild ride to find the truth.

God began the journey by poking holes in what the men of the East had always believed.  He pointed at specific examples Job and his friends used as evidence for their reward-and-punishment theology and slowly eroded their conclusions.

For instance, in Job 9:2-13, Job makes some weighty accusations against the way that God works:

> Indeed, I know that this is true.  But how can mere mortals prove their innocence before God?  Though they wished to dispute with him, they could not answer him one time out of a thousand.  His wisdom is profound, his power is vast.  Who has resisted him and come out unscathed?  He moves mountains without their knowing it and overturns them in his anger.  He shakes the earth from its place and makes its pillars tremble.  He speaks to the sun and it does not shine; he seals off the light of the stars.  He alone stretches out

the heavens and treads on the waves of the sea. He is the Maker of the Bear and Orion, the Pleiades and the constellations of the south. He performs wonders that cannot be fathomed, miracles that cannot be counted. When he passes me, I cannot see him; when he goes by, I cannot perceive him. If he snatches away, who can stop him? Who can say to him, 'What are you doing?' God does not restrain his anger; even the cohorts of Rahab cowered at his feet. (NIV)

This is exactly where God started. He took these very examples and questioned Job's conclusion that God does not restrain His anger and even His worst enemies should cower at His feet.

First, He asked Job about how he got his firsthand knowledge. If it wasn't actually firsthand, did he really know how and why things work? Let's look at what God started out asking. (I am paraphrasing His questions for time and space. Turn to Job 38 for the full conversation.)

"Were you there at creation?"

Job's internal answer would have to be, no. He knew nothing about the pillars or foundations of the earth by firsthand knowledge.

"Do you know why the sea behaves like it does?"

No, Job had implied that the sea splashes in waves because God is stomping around and disturbing them. God is questioning Job's conclusions about waves.

"Do you know how the sun rises each morning?"

No, not really, though Job claimed God turned out the lights whenever He wanted.

"Do you know how the earth's crust got its shape?"

No.

"So, do you know how I handle the wicked?" No.

"Do you know the secrets of death and the dark places?" No.

"If you know everything there is to know on earth let's hear it. Can you tell me where light and dark come from since you're so wise and aged?" No.

Job quickly remembered that being the wisest, greatest man in all the East didn't mean that he knew all there was to know. While he and his friends thought they had it all worked out, they really knew so little of how things actually worked. God was shaking up the absolutes Job believed so strongly.

The next little bit is interesting. Before we read it, let's look back at another belief held by the men of the East:

> The tempest comes out from its chamber, the cold from the driving winds. The breath of God produces ice, and the broad waters become frozen. He loads the clouds with moisture; he scatters his lightning through them. At his direction they swirl around over the face of the whole earth to do whatever he commands them. He brings the clouds to punish people, or to water his earth and show his love.   (Job 37:9-13, NIV)

Apparently, at this point in history the Middle East had drastically different weather than today. Though it does snow there in winter, large bodies of water no longer freeze solid. It does however sound like a great description of the immense storms the earth would have experienced as a result of the ice age following the judgment of the Great Flood. We know from genealogies, Job was born only about 600-700 years after the Flood when it was still fresh on humanity's mind. This Flood was the standard of how Job and his friends believed God dealt with the earth. Bad=spanking. Good=love and blessing. I can hear the parents and clergy of his day spinning the Flood story to scare children into behaving in the same way some parents today use the Boogeyman or even Santa. Don't be naughty, or God will wipe you out.

God asked how they knew this grandiose caricature of Him was true:

> "Have you been to the place where I store all this pent up judgment you've been describing? Have you seen the storehouses of snow and hail?"

Job's answer would again have to be no. In fact, there's no such thing as a storehouse for snow or hail; Job could never have seen it. God does not have a safety deposit box in the sky where every time you sin He puts in a chunk of ice just waiting for the opportune time to dump it out. God is asking a question in order to get Job thinking about why he has made assumptions about God's judgment. He's questioning Job's proof for what he believes. God's not making a statement that there are storehouses for snow, literal or figurative. The implication of God's question is not to affirm Job's way of thinking, but to get Job to question why he believes what he does. The conclusion is that since Job doesn't know how everything else works he may not understand how judgment works either.

God keeps Job's mind moving forward:

> "Who cuts a channel for the torrents of rain, and a path for the thunderstorm, to water a land where no one lives, an uninhabited desert, to satisfy a desolate wasteland and make it sprout with grass?" (NIV)

What an astounding question! To us it may seem like a simple thing; duh, it rains. But for Job it must have felt like an explosion in his brain. They had just been talking about how God sent the rain to love or punish. Had they ever stopped to think about why it rains in a place where no one lives? If God does what He does solely for reward and punishment, then why does He bless a land where there isn't a soul to incur reward or punishment? There is a strong contrast between their assumption about judgment and what God was trying to show them.

Why does it rain in places where no one lives? Job did not know. The answer is the global weather system. God created the "firmament" (Gen 1:6-8). In the majority of situations, God has set up physiological laws which govern the weather. Each raindrop is in the process of evaporation or condensation. Job accused God of micro-managing things that God had, for the most part, delegated to systems. For some reason we do not blame God's magical powers when the law of gravity pulls an exploding space shuttle back to earth; we get that laws are at work. But if a storm comes, the laws of thermodynamics are not a sufficient explanation. We call it an "act of God." God can and does intervene in his systems, but most often the systems simply follow the laws He set up to run them.

The problem is that many of these systems were broken because of the curse. They now swing to extremes as the system tries to find equilibrium. Droughts, floods, and earthquakes are now common, not because God is punishing or rewarding but because the earth's perfection is lost.

Many of God's questions to this point have to do with the powerful forces of creation, the catastrophic changes from the flood, and the resulting chaos. Job looked at these forces as proof that God is powerful, angry, and vengeful. He is the giver and the one who takes away. Job did not have enough information. There is more to the equation than bad equals spanking.

God is just. He holds the balance of justice in His hands. An earth burning with violence must be quenched. God's balance of justice determined that at the time of the Flood, justice must act with enough force to counterbalance evil and save the innocent. God intervened in the global weather system and sent the Flood. (It wouldn't surprise me if some sort of scene like what happened in Job 1-2 also happened before the flood, hidden from view.)

However, that does not mean that because God used the weather for a very specific purpose that every snowflake, raindrop, or hail stone since then is an act of judgment. In fact, He promised never to do that on a global scale again. Our everyday weather is typically a sign that God loves His creation enough to design a well balanced system for precipitation and temperature that allows life to thrive and grow regardless of whether we have done good or bad (Acts 14:17, Matt 5:43-48).

God generated all life. He loves life. He *is* life (Jn. 14:6). He would rather we all turn from the way that leads to death and choose life without the need for Him to intervene in a dramatic way (Duet 30:19, Prov 16:25, Ezek 18, Ezek 33). Punishing us is not His evening entertainment!

Because they attempted to label everything that happens as positive or negative feedback from God about our behavior, Job and his friends didn't believe you could have a relationship with the Lofty Judge. They said things like:

"Thick clouds veil him, so he does not see us as he goes about in the vaulted heavens." (Eliphaz quoted Job in 22:14, NIV)

The Chiefs of the East had determined He brings catastrophe to punish the wicked and comfort to bless the righteous. That's only one set of variables in the equation of justice. Our value to God, even in our broken state, is another weighty factor. Job was completely missing God's indiscriminate love. Therefore, his conclusions were faulty, otherwise why did God send rain on a place no one lives?

God's actions are not solely dependent on what we do or don't do; they are a matter of His character. Though God has used rain as both a reward and a punishment, not every single drop of rain is an act of justice. We need to back up and look at the context of the bigger picture rather than just trying to understand why one raindrop falls. God says He provides for the land where no one lives. He uses the global weather system to water the earth regardless of man's activities. The rain falls because God was wise enough to invent a system that governs the weather.

In fact, like most things that God set in motion, it can be over simplified: Water evaporates. When there's enough, it will get too heavy and fall back down. However, for those who are mature enough to try to work out the equation needed in order to predict when and where the rain will fall, they need giant super-computers to run fancy algorithms. Even then they are not right all of the time because there are so many variables and still so much the experts don't know or understand.

This is exactly the problem of trying to predict when and where bad things will happen. We try to use our kindergarten understanding of sowing and reaping to predict the outcome of a complex system of justice that has more layers than the atmosphere and more variables than the Jet Stream. God cannot be reduced to a formula with neat, square boxes.

Proverbs 8 tells us that God created the Wisdom of all knowable things then used it to create the world (see especially vs. 22-31). Before He made anything tangible, God created mathematics, sciences, the arts, laws of logic, and the moral codes, et cetera. With them He set the worlds in motion. The last step for setting things in motion was to create man to govern the earth (Gen 1). Then God rested from creating new systems (Gen 2:1-3). His plan was to maintain and expand the systems through a relationship with humanity (Gen 1:26). He even indwelt us with His Spirit of Wisdom (Gen 2:7), but by choosing to reject Him we cut off that essential relationship. We are now living in the world that resulted from our poor governorship without Him (Gen 3).

Though He set systems in motion, He is not a far off God who started everything and then stepped away. No, He is seeking to restore our broken relationship. He's carefully watching what's going on and diligently listening to our prayers (Ps 33:13-14, 69:33). The outcome of every decision is predictable to Him. He is constantly weighing the outcomes and working within these now broken systems for the good of creation. His balance of justice determines when He will act to intervene in the systems and when He will not. We will see this more clearly as God's answer progresses.

What could Job have determined by answering all the questions God has asked thus far? Though I have drawn many conclusions by observing results in creation and hearing the history of the world passed down to me, I do not actually know how or why things were created to work. God knows because He created everything. He knows how, why, when, how much, how far... He knows the motives because the motives are His.

Until his encounter with God, Job had only been guessing at the way the world works and what motivates God by looking at the results around him. He had some good reasons to believe what he did about God and the universe. You see, Job was living right next door to Israel in the Land of Uz. Lamentations tells us that the people who lived in Uz were called Edomites (Lam 4:21). That meant Job was a descendant of Abraham on the black sheep side of the family. Edom is another name for Esau (Gen 25). Esau was one-half of the famous twins Jacob and Esau, born to Isaac son of Abraham. Though he was the eldest, Esau was rejected as the heir to the Promise. He sold that birthright to Jacob for a bowl of red lentil stew. Jacob went on to steal their father's blessing too. God had predicted it all before the boys were even born. This would have had a huge impact on Job's theology. God would seem legalistically judgmental on one hand and arbitrarily cruel on the other. Yet God was good to Abraham because he obeyed. These three attributes seem to be the basis of Job's belief system. God rewarded the obedient and punished the wicked. But God was also supreme and could do anything He wanted on a whim, so watch out for stray lightning bolts!

Some scholars even go so far as to say that Job and Jobab on the genealogy lists found in Genesis 36 and 1 Chronicles 1 are the same person. While it might be a bit of a rabbit trail to follow this idea, if true, it sheds some light on the dynamics between Job and his friends, which in turn sheds light on Job's views on authority, and ultimately God.

A little context first: Esau married three women. Two wives were local Hittites (Gen 26:34-35). One was Oholibama (also known as Judith, probably a title she earned as a seer). She was the daughter of a local big shot, Anah. The other wife was Adah (aka Basemath; she had to change her name because Esau married another girl with the same name).

Adah's father, Elon, probably owned the oak groves used in worshiping local gods, another powerful man. Together these women caused his momma grief, so Esau went out and got a third wife from among the family (Gen 28:9). This wife, Mahalath (aka Basemath), was the daughter of Ishmael, Abraham's oldest son. While not a perfect choice, she was at least part of the family, not some disagreeable foreigner his mother hated. The important bit in all this back story is that Esau had one son, Reuel, with the wife approved of by his parents. King Jobab was the grandson of Reuel. King Jobab probably inherited the family fortune because the children from Esau's first two wives were judged inferior because of their mothers. It was totally unfair—he was the baby, but got everything just like with Jacob and Esau.

There's another layer to that story which makes Jobab's inheritance even more appalling. Esau's Father-in-Law Anah was important because he discovered the precious springs in the wilderness. (For those actually looking up the verses in Genesis, he later changed his name to Beeri meaning "my well"; his identity was tied to the power owning this water gave him). If life were fair, Anah's grandsons should have gotten his wells, not this Jobab kid. Instead, because of family prejudice, possession passed to young Jobab giving a Semite great power in the Hittite land. He became the king of Edom, the greatest man in all the East. In fact, the land of Uz, originally named after Anah's grandson Uz, soon became known as the Land of Edom named after Jobab's people.

Jobab was from a city in Uz called Bozrah. The city's remains have been found near the modern city of Bouseira, Jordan. Bozrah means "fold." A fold is a place where animals are kept, like a sheepfold. It would have been fitting for a man who owned as many animals as Job to be from a town named Bozrah. This is one of the reasons I think the correlation between Job and Jobab might be true.

If it's true, then Job's friend Eliphaz was really his great-uncle, first born of all Esau's seemingly not-good-enough kids. That would make several of their jabs at each other make more sense. Eliphaz was truly wise and aged (Job15:10), while Job may have been as young as forty give or take a few years (especially considering he had ten more kids and lived another 140 years after all this).

We also know Job's friend Zophar was from a nearby Palestinian city named Naamah not to far from the border of Edom (Josh 15:41). Bildad was a Shuhite descended from one of Abraham's sons by Keturah whom he married after Sarah died (Gen 25:2). The young man named Elihu was a Buzite which would make him a descendant of Abraham's nephew by his brother Nahor (Gen 22:21).

All were related to Abraham, but not from the line of the "chosen heir" Jacob. These rejected offspring got together and had discussions of the nature of God. They came to conclusions that everybody had known "since mankind was placed on the earth" (Job 20:4), knowledge passed down from the "former generations" (Job 8:8, 15:18). All these men believed that relationship with God was only for a chosen few, and they were not it. They needed to earn God's blessing.

Job had heard his family and world histories. He had heard about God, but he'd not met Him personally. He'd been reverse engineering the motives of the most complex Being in the universe from rumors and circumstance. In Job's eyes, God was definitely prejudiced and harsh. How could there be any other conclusion from all of this evidence?

God was challenging these very assumptions. After disassembling Job's confidence in everything he thought he knew, God moved on to the next series of questions. He veered from poking at what Job knew and began to ask what power or right he had to set the rules of the universe. Just because he was king, the greatest in the East, did Job have the power of God? The questions start with things like "can you?" or "do you?" instead of "have you seen?" or "where were you when?"

"Can you affect the constellations?"

No. Who does? God does.

"Do you have power to control the weather?"

No, God does.

"Can you count the clouds?"

No, but God can.

Job may not have thought he ruled the world, but he definitely accused God of doing it wrong. He was now faced with the reality that he does not have the power to set his own standards of justice. His accusations that God was failing in His duty to punish the wicked and bless the righteous were misguided. Though Job is the greatest in the East, he is not *the* Greatest. God is the only one with the power to rule the world. He does not do so according to Job's ways, but according to something much bigger than man's way of thinking. By the end of these questions Job's theology is in shambles and his world view is turned upside down.

Previously, when I had read the Book of Job, I thought that the whole four chapters of God's answer were to point out the obvious fact that Job was little compared the Almighty. Job clearly didn't know as much as God. Yet I wondered why God would belittle Job's insufficiency, especially in his current condition? It seemed so hateful and cruel. I empathized with Job because it felt like my world was caving in too. God seemed just like Job's friends, the guys Job just wanted to shut up. If God felt that way toward the greatest man in the East, then I must truly be a wretched worm in His sight. I had no chance of happiness again. God had no answers to offer, just sovereign supremacy.

But, that's not it at all. Job did need to realize just how off target his theology was, but God doesn't simply grind on that one point for four chapters. He accomplished what He set out to do and then moved on to a new set of ideas to bring about Job's change of thinking. This next part is juicy and wonderful—and it just keeps getting better!

Chapter 5

The Lioness and the Raven

"Do you hunt the prey for the lioness and satisfy the hunger of the lions when they crouch in their dens or lie in wait in a thicket?" (Job 38:39-40, NIV)

So far God showed Job that he does not know everything, nor does he have the power to run the world. God then began to build a picture of how He actually does interact with His creation. He moved from talking about the elements to talking about what Job knew best: animals. God focused on wild things outside of Job's care. They're creatures Job would have seen as useless competition at best, and as feared enemy at worst. They were obstacles to Job's profit. God used Job's knowledge about these outliers to illustrate how He treats those who refuse to obey Him and spurn His loving care.

As we saw with creation and the global weather system, God did not select arbitrary topics. He responded directly to Job's use of animals as proof that God punishes bad guys and rewards the good. For example, in chapter 12 Job says:

> But ask the animals, and they will teach you, or the birds in the sky, and they will tell you; or speak to the earth, and it will teach you, or let the fish in the sea inform you. Which of all these does not know that the

hand of the Lord has done this?  In his hand is the life of every creature and the breath of all mankind. (NIV)

God used these animals to illustrate the truth just as Job used them as evidence of his false conclusions.  If you want more specific examples, re-read Job 26 before we continue to look deeper at God's answer.

If there was one subject God could use to help Job understand, it was this. God didn't need a lot of explanation on each topic.  Job would have known instantly the characteristics of each of the animals.  After all, Job's massive herds are a big reason he's considered the greatest man in the East.  They were his living, and he was really good at it.

We on the other hand have a disadvantage to understanding the story.  Few of us are familiar with as many animals as Job.  We will need to put ourselves in Job's shoes. Imagine each animal:  what it would represent in Job's era, how does it act, what's its reputation, and what is the way Job said God should deal with those types of actions?  It might help you imagine the significance of each animal if you pull it up on your search engine.

God begins with a creature Job must have loathed, the lion. It was a livestock killer.  Its very existence was contrary to Job's wealth, wellbeing, and safety.  It should have been a good example of what God does to wicked people.

Before we get to God's question, let's look at how Job's friend Eliphaz references lions:

> Consider now: Who, being innocent, has ever perished?  Where were the upright ever destroyed?  As I have observed, those who plow evil and those who sow trouble reap it.  At the breath of God they perish; at the blast of his anger they are no more.  The lions

may roar and growl, yet the teeth of the great lions are broken. The lion perishes for lack of prey, and the cubs of the lioness are scattered. (Job 4:7-11, NIV)

Eliphaz is illustrating the point that God rages against those who do evil. He will bust their teeth right out of their heads. They will starve to death, permanently disabled from their terrible beating, no longer able to maintain their dominion. It would take no more than the breath of God to bring about the destruction of those who think they are mighty.

Job used lions as an illustration in chapter 10. He says:

If I sinned, you would be watching me and would not let my offense go unpunished. If I am guilty—woe to me! Even if I am innocent, I cannot lift my head, for I am full of shame and drowned in my affliction. If I hold my head high, you stalk me like a lion and again display your awesome power against me. You bring new witnesses against me and increase your anger toward me; your forces come against me wave upon wave. (Job 10:14-17, NIV)

Job said God stalked him like a lion stalking prey. It didn't matter whether he was guilty or innocent. God roars and everyone is afraid. God swaggers like the king of the beasts. He shows the world His might by crushing those who stand out in a crowd with their heads held high. Job feels like a poor impala out for an evening of innocent grazing when God—WHAM!—pounces and mauls him to death.

Let's contrast these ideas with what God says about the lion:

Do you hunt the prey for the lioness and satisfy the hunger of the lions when they crouch in their dens or lie in wait in a thicket? (NIV)

This question is similar to the question of why it rains where no one lives. It is a simple question with profound implications. Job was only focused on the punishment of the violent; God asks about their provision. If God only punishes bad and rewards good, who provides for the lion?

Does Job provide food for the lion? No, not in any form or fashion. In a shepherd's view, extermination is the only good end for the lion. In fact, lions are extinct in the Middle East due largely to this very reason. From a strictly humanist perspective, maybe Job would be justified in looking out for the best interest of himself and his livestock; so many people depend on him for life. Kill the lions!

Job felt the same way about carnivorous humans. In Job's estimation such a morally depraved creature was worthy of severe consequences. They should be eradicated to leave more room for the good guys. In Job 21:19-21 he clearly states how he believed God should deal with those who refuse to live according to God's ways. They should die for their misdeeds swiftly and without mercy. There should be no question about their fate.

Does God deal with the lion according to Job's methods? No, not even carnivores are hated by God. In fact, these wild creatures are given basic freedoms to make a living regardless of their relationship to the Creator.

God did not hunt the prey for the lions either. But He did create a suitable environment with sunshine, water cycles, and the plant growth cycle. This in turn drives the migration cycle and brings new prey to the lion's territory. God gave the lion strength, intelligence, and community within the pride, etc. In other words, He put systems in place to provide a way for the lion to thrive.

In addition to these autonomic systems, God also provided for the lion when He charged humanity with the conscious, voluntary task of caring for lions. God commissioned man to oversee and care for the beasts of the field and everything that moves on four legs—including lions (Gen 1:24-28). We are supposed to do this in His likeness and image so that when others look at us, they will know exactly what He is like.

Does God feel the same as Job about fallen people? No. In Matthew 5, Jesus tells us God's way of treating His enemies very clearly:

> But I tell you, love your enemies and pray for those who persecute you, that you may be children of your Father in heaven. He causes his sun to rise on the evil and the good, and sends rain on the righteous and the unrighteous. If you love those who love you, what reward will you get? Are not even the tax collectors doing that? And if you greet only your own people, what are you doing more than others? Do not even pagans do that? Be perfect, therefore, as your heavenly Father is perfect. (Matt 5:44-48, NIV)

Love for ones enemies is the most sacred, holy perfection. It sets God apart from all others. It is the characteristic He desires for us to emulate the most (Matt 22:37-40).

God was not there to break the teeth of the proud, self-satisfied lion as Eliphaz portrayed Him. Neither was He hunting Job for sport. If God loves lions enough to provide what they need to make a life, He would do the same for Job.

God asked this question about the lion to point out the contrast between His true character and the Chiefs' assumptions about Him. God does not control the lion's every move. He does not beat it and force it to be kind and follow the rules. In fact, the lion lives contrary to the peaceful, vegetarian world God created and called good (Gen 1:30-31). Even so, God provided the lion with an alternative to a civilized existence and a habitat for it to make a living. Lions are alive and thriving. Therefore, God does not simply annihilate violent men as Job assumed He should.

Out there in the kingdom of this world, the rules are eat or be eaten and survival of the fittest. It isn't an easy life. Lions don't enjoy all the luxuries of a prized house kitty; they are wild cats in the wilderness scratching out a living. The trials that face these wild beasts are not necessarily punishment directly from the hand of God, but are instead the result of living in a fallen world.

The lion is not outside of God's compassion; it's just living according to the rules of a dog-eat-dog world. Yet even in the wilderness, survival of the fittest isn't the only rule; there is also a system of laws which govern its existence and determine its destiny. Laws such as: everything moves from order to chaos unless an outside force—like us—intervenes, for every action there is an equal and opposite reaction, you reap what you sow, etc. Laws are there to keep balance and equilibrium in a chaotic system. They set limits as to how far we can go before a major correction swings things back in the other direction.

Does God ever intervene in the systems that govern the lion's welfare? Yes, but not usually. God is very much aware of every lion, what their needs are, and the needs of every other animal in the territory. Yet He mostly leaves intervention up to us, to care for them in His name. It was the job He gave us at the very beginning, and our commission has never been revoked, not even when humanity sinned. Humanity is still His only heir to this earth (Rom 4:13-17). We are supposed to intervene in the entropy we see around us. As the world decays, we are to build, protect, and repair. We are not supposed to only look out for our own good, but also the good of the whole earth. God encourages humanity to love and care. This is how we "take dominion over the earth" (see Gen 1:28).

In the same way that God governs and provides for the lion, God governs those who choose to be distant from Him. He does not control our every move. We have a choice to be in the kingdom of God under His direct care where He can tend our wounds and give us aide and comfort. Or we can be out there in the kingdom of this world, living under the rules of the systems He created. Either way God still expects those of us who claim to be His children to intervene on behalf of those who are suffering. We have even more responsibility for His two legged creations than with the four legged variety.

Living in the wilderness is not the whole answer as to why bad things happen. The full answer is much more complex, and after a few more examples we will try to be more thorough. This is just our first baby step away from the concept that all bad things that happen are a direct result of God punching somebody's teeth out. Someday everything will be set right; the lion and the lamb will once again get along (Isa 11& 65). But for now that is not the case. The lion is a carnivore and will be until the curse is gone.

It was a simple question: Who provides for the hungry lion? Job probably didn't get the point from this one example. The question may have just got him thinking. But God keeps asking more and more questions with the same conclusions until finally it becomes clear. God loves and values His enemies. He always has, not just in the New Testament, but always. This is just the beginning of turning a theology that has been set on the same destructive course for generations. Like a slowly turning ship, it has only moved one degree from where it was heading before, but it will eventually do a full about-face.

After the lion, God brings up the raven:

> "Who provides food for the raven when its young cry out to God and wander about for lack of food?" (Job 38:41, NIV)

Does Job provide for the raven when its young cry out? No.

What kind of a bird is a raven? It is a disgusting, loud mouthed, smarty-pants, bad omen, thief, pest, and scavenger. Imagine what it eats, how it eats. You've seen them feasting on road kill and its maggots or stealing from a farmer's field and trash. This would have been infuriating and disgusting to Job and more so to the kosher Jewish audience for whom the story was written down. Eating raw, dead carcasses makes it truly foul.

According to Job's philosophy, should anyone as filthy and revolting such as this bird receive any aid? No. According to Job what should happen to a no-good scallywag? Zap! Yet God loves and cares for this creature, answering its chick's prayer for food.

It reminds me of a couple of other New Testament teachings. "Consider the ravens: They do not sow or reap, they have no storeroom or barn; yet God feeds them. And how much more valuable you are than birds!" (Luke 12:24, NIV). Think also of the parable about sparrows. Since God loves and cares for sparrows which are only worth a penny per pair, then imagine how much more He loves and cares for humanity. If God clothes the lily more beautifully than Solomon, how much more will He take care of us (Matt 10)?

Like the lion, the raven is wild and lives according to the system of laws that govern balance in the wilderness. But

God points out one important reason He will intervene in the system of laws. "Its young cry out to God."

Psalm 147:9 says, "He [God] provides food for the cattle and for the young ravens when they call."

Crying out to God in prayer is the first step for beginning a relationship with Him. We don't have to be perfect to pray! We can talk to Him just as we are. He wants to hear even from people society has rejected as outcasts. He wants a relationship even with ravens.

I do not fully understand prayer. Sometimes I have seen God intervene and provide exactly what I asked Him for. Other times (usually after the fact) I've seen how He provided something that I actually needed rather than what I asked. And sometimes I've seen Him use the very thing I was trying to avoid in order to provide freedom that I would never have had otherwise.

God hears our call and provides exactly what we need, not necessarily what we want. It's a good thing to call out to Him with our physical needs. But don't be surprised if He gives us the Bread of Life or Living Water, rather than the temporary substitutes we think we want (John 4:1-26, 6:1-60).

Sometimes God intervenes in the systems simply because His compassion is aroused when He sees us "wandering about for lack of food" (Hos 11:8, Ps 72:12-14). We go about like sheep without a shepherd (Mark 6:34). We are eaten and crushed because humanity fails to follow the laws in the kingdom of God, or our authorities neglect their duties. God's heart is moved at our pain (Exod 3:7).

To us it may seem like there is no rhyme or reason to when God's balance of justice tips in favor of victims and when it leans in favor of offenders who have not earned His compassion. It may seem hard to see why sometimes He acts out of His mercy, and sometimes He allows the rules to arbitrate our consequences. I assure you there is both reason and law, compassion and pity. All God's decisions are motivated by His love for creation. It is the one constant when trying to understand why God does what He does when He does it. The pattern will become more clear as we continue to look at the examples God provides.

One thing is certain; God causes blessing on the righteous and just as well as the unrighteous and the unjust (Matt 5:43-48). God loved and died for us all while we were sinners (Rom 5:8). There is never a point at which we are good enough to earn His blessing. If blessing worked like scales, we would always be lacking. Job viewed the Almighty as a mountain who crushed everyone without regard (see Job 9). The truth is that God gives good gifts without regard. Thank God He cares for those like the lion and the raven. How wonderful He is! How great must our God be to know when to act on our behalf and when we will grow more through trouble! There is no God like Him who loves and cares for His enemies.

Likewise, perfectly reflecting God the Father requires us to love our enemies and pray for their good. God is kind even to those who do not deserve it. The deepest question we can ask ourselves when we see trouble in the world is not "why," but instead "are we fulfilling God's Genesis 1 edict to rule over the earth in God's image as His likeness?"

For the most part, the answer is no. We tend to either turn our commission into Gaia worship where the earth is more important than the people for whom it was created, or we abuse the earth for our own profit regardless of our responsibility for its future. It ends up looking like anarchy or totalitarianism. At either extreme the image of God we portray is warped and broken.

Humanity has utterly fallen short of being the exact representation of who God is. I believe a huge reason for that is that God's image has been warped and twisted to look like the same old god that Job had pictured: an angry, tyrannical, far off consumer. That is really the image of Satan.

That is not how God treats either the lion or the raven. He provides for them in many ways even though to Job they were the enemy. God does not micro-manage their choices, nor does He crush them at their first offence. They are given space to live free in the wild—for a time.

When trying to understand God's goodness in situations like these, we need to take into account the broader scope of creation. There may be a terrible "butterfly effect" we can't even comprehend if God intervenes in our situation the way we demand. We need to stop focusing only on what we think is best for ourselves and our small world. Instead we need to start regarding our enemies plight just as much as our own.

This is the beginning of a new way of thinking. God prepared Job's heart with a warning that it would be a radical shift from his old theology. Nothing could be farther from what Job had always heard about God. I hope Job had found a way to put on his big boy pants. Otherwise, he may have been freaking out at this point.

God affirmed the facts that had confused and frustrated Job. God is not sitting on His throne in heaven in a long white beard waiting to zap people with lightning bolts. (That is actually the image of a false god named Zeus.) God's throne is in heaven, but He's more the type of God who "hovers over the surface of the waters" (Gen 1:1). He is watching. But, He is watching with the intent to do what is best for us. Is it best for Him to act or not to act? God is the best one to answer that question, not us from our limited point of view, our limited reasoning, and our limited compassion for our enemy.

God takes care of the bad guy! Why would He do that? How is that right? Why should I ever be good again? If such grace is available regardless of my actions, why bother following the rules!?

Don't worry, this isn't the end of the answer; there is more to it. God brings it all around in the end. There is justice in the world. There is order to the world. There is a purpose for the rules. There is a reason to follow them. Right now, God is breaking Job free from the old theological mold that says God loves us when we obey and hates us when we don't.

He is allowing Job to see that his value to God does not come from his ability to obey. He is more than just the sum of his actions. He is a creature created by God. Loved by God. Provided for by God. Not because he earned it, but because it is the character of God to do so. God is the Self-Sufficient Sustainer of all that is.

Chapter 6

The Mountain Goat

"Do you know when the mountain goats give birth?  ...They crouch down and bring forth their young; their labor pains are ended." (Job 38:1a, 3, NIV)

The next creature God brought up for review is the mountain goat.  Though it was wild, it wasn't disgusting or cruel like the previous two animals.  Why did He mention it?

Job was going through anguish.  He said more than once that he wished God would just smite him dead.  His life had been rich.  Now that it wasn't, he felt like he was going to die like a heathen.  He never looked beyond the pain of the moment to see that things had the potential to change.  He thought God hated him, and that was going to be the end of it all:

> Isn't mankind consigned to forced labor on earth?  Are not his days like those of a hired hand?  Like a slave he longs for shade; like a hired man he waits for his pay. So I have been made to inherit months of futility, and troubled nights have been assigned to me. When I lie down I think: When will I get up? But the evening drags on endlessly, and I toss and turn until dawn. My flesh is clothed with maggots and encrusted with dirt. My skin forms scabs and oozes. My

days pass more swiftly than a weaver's shuttle; they come to an end without hope. Remember that my life is but a breath. My eye will never again see anything good. The eye of anyone who looks on me will no longer see me. Your eyes will look for me, but I will be gone. As a cloud fades away and vanishes, so the one who goes down to Sheol will never rise again. He will never return to his house; his hometown will no longer remember him. Therefore I will not restrain my mouth. I will speak in the anguish of my spirit; I will complain in the bitterness of my soul. (Job 7:1-11, HCSB)

With the wild goat, God acknowledges Job's pain and gets him thinking about it in a different way. By talking through His relationship to the wild mountain goat, He offered great comfort to the hurting man.

Because of his experience with animals, Job didn't need back information about the wild goat. He and God could just jump right into discussing it. Since most of us have no idea exactly what creature God is talking about, let's start by learning a little about it.

Based on the area of the world in which Job lived and the similarity of behaviors described, the wild goat was probably something like the Nubian Ibex which still ranges the Middle East and northern parts of Africa.

This stately animal prefers to live high up on the formidable, rocky cliffs moving from place to place to find patches of grass and small scrub brush to eat. It can walk easily in places no sane human would dare try to scale without special equipment. Due to the extremely inhospitable terrain, it can be difficult to observe their elusive behavior.

The females conceive sometime in October and November. When their time comes, they go off alone away from the herd to give birth, finding shelter in crags and caves. The kids are born in the spring mostly between March and May. Healthy young are able to leap and run on the rocks within a day of birth.

Keeping all of this in mind here is what God asks Job next:

> Do you know the time the mountain goat gives birth? While the doe labors in the craggy rocks, do you keep watch? Do you count the months until her time is fulfilled? Do you know the time she delivers? She crouches down, her offspring pierces through, and then she casts away the cord. They grow plump and multiply on grass seed. They leave and do not return. (Job 39:1-4)

Job would probably have been too busy with the birth of his own goats to bother thinking about the wild herds. Yet God implies He has a certain level of intimacy with this wild creature.

He has watched each doe as she bears her kid—even in the craggiest of rocks. Not only did He see her in her time of trouble, He knew the day she conceived. He counted everyday while her baby grew inside her. He knew what she felt every time her kid kicked and wriggled. He knew before she did when she would begin the pain of contractions. He knew where she would shelter for the birth and saw her when it happened. There's nowhere she could have hidden from Him, nor did she need to.

What would this mean to a man who was going through his own time of trouble, who felt like he was in agony? It would have spoken directly to his hurting heart.

Yes, God is watching over you. He knows every intimate detail of your pain—even more than you can understand about it yourself. From the time it was conceived until the time it has fully developed, He has been aware of every detail of what you are going through. He has not forgotten you. Though you think He's watching you like a lion ready to pounce, He has no such ill intent. There is no reason for you to hide your pain from Him. There is no where you can go that He is not there for you. Kindness and care in times of pain is the nature of God's attention.

It reminds me of the slave girl named Hagar that Sarah gave to Abraham to be a surrogate mother. When Hagar found out she was pregnant, she despised Sarah. Sarah retaliated bitterly.

Hagar was afraid, so she ran away. We find in Genesis 16 that as she wept by a well in the desert, God called her by name. He gave her both comfort and a promise. He told her that her son would become a great people. She believed Him and gave God a name, "El Roi." It means "The God Who Sees." She named the well there "Beer Lahai Roi" which means "the well of the Living One who sees me." She gave her son the name "Ishmael" which means "God hears."

She took comfort in the fact that even in the desert God could see her pain and heard her cry. He knew what was happening between her and her mistress. He could offer guidance when the way seemed impossible. She trusted Him and obeyed by going back to live with Abraham and Sarah.

Sometimes God's intervention is not at all what we hope for. God did not force the people in her life to treat her nicely or make her the princess instead of her mistress. But He did provide exactly what she needed when she cried out in her time of trouble. Abraham's descendents are still reaping the effects of the war between Sarah and Hagar.  God provides, even for His potential enemies.

Like Hagar and the mountain goat, God does not leave us alone in our pain.  Do not be afraid; you are not alone in the wilderness with no one to help you.  Though there are times in life we feel abandoned and thirsty, God can bring us through.  Cry out to Him.

Many of us have a tendency to withdraw and hide our pain.  Like the mountain goat in labor, we shrink into the crags and caves.  However, we are not ibex.  As humans, we are not meant to be alone in our time of trouble.  We not only have the opportunity to cry out to God, but also to each other.  Galatians 6 tells us, "Bear one another's burdens, and thereby fulfill the law of Christ" (NASB).  It is often fear of judgment or ridicule that causes us to hide our pain from others.  In the family of God, this should not be the case.  We are to love and care for each other.  We are meant to share each others' burdens and help each other through life.

In 2 Corinthians 1, Paul tells us that God is the Father of mercies and God of all comfort.   He comforts us in our affliction so that we will be able to comfort others with the comfort we receive.  God is there for us, and we can be there for others.

Besides pointing out His attentiveness, God also made another affectionate point with the wild goat.  He said, "They crouch down and bring forth their young; their labor pains are ended.  Their young thrive and grow strong in the wilds; they leave and do not return" (NIV).

The doe went through the pain of labor, but the labor ended when she gave birth.  Compare that with Job who felt like the heartache he was going through was going to last for the rest of his life.  He wished he could just die and get it over with.  If the doe thought the same thing when she went into labor, she would never get through it. Yes, she may never have been the same again; she may even have had permanent scars from the process. Yet the hope of what was on the other side made all the pain worth it. In the end she had everything she desired. She was able to fulfill her purpose, her destiny. In the process she helped the herd to stay strong and healthy.

Heartache does not have to be the end of life abundantly. Trust that God can see you through to the other side of this trial. We may change and even bear scars from our ordeals. But these marks in our lives do not have to be the last word in our story, just a heart racing chapter. God can use the painful seasons to be the catalysts we need to give birth to our life's purpose. Most of us do not give in to change without a fight; this trial may just be the fight we need to win in order to bring peace that passes all understanding. We will never know if we give up in the middle of it. We need to persevere to the end like Job who eventually found the joy and honor he had been pursuing all along.

Birth was never intended to be such a traumatic experience. God made the first humans already mature. He set them up in paradise then came to walk with them in the cool of the evening. A relationship with God is supposed to be free, open, and un-traumatic. God said it was very good—until we chose to mess it up.

Genesis 3:16 tells us that one of the consequences of the curse is pain in labor and child rearing. It wasn't created to be a painful process. He is not watching over the ibex to cause the pain of labor. It hurts so much because of the choice Eve made. We live in a fallen world. Now pain is something we go through to reach maturity.

I think this is in part because maturity is the ability to voluntarily make good choices. We are often stumbling through the learning process on our own accord, learning by trial and error. We tend to make the choice that protects our bubble rather than the choice that will make us stronger and more mature. We often don't choose to progress on our own accord. But like a baby on its due date, the bubble eventually needs to pop, or we will die. There is a natural process where strong forces are applied to push us out of our comfort zone. We don't realize how much more there is to life until we are forced beyond the limits of our current, dark understanding.

The analogy of life's troubles to labor pains is great, but it only deals with the last obvious stages of its birth. It doesn't explain the conception or growth of the trial we are in. We may be able to trace it back through months of symptoms like Braxton Hicks and morning sickness of the soul. But often all we remember of the beginning was being blissfully unaware that trouble was brewing.

It is natural to search for the root of why things happen. That's what most of us were looking for when we opened the Book of Job.

With the wild goat, God saw even the mysterious beginning of conception. God was also there in the court of heaven when Job was put on trial. He knew the conception of the matter. He could easily have explained to Job about Satan's accusations and the proceedings that followed, but that is not the information God thought was important to Job's healing and growth.

The root of Job's struggle was not the trial in heaven; it was his misunderstanding of the merciful character of God. Therefore, God sought to reveal Himself to Job, not answer why the mess was happening.

There are many things going on behind the scenes of our lives as well. These things each have an effect on our circumstances. The "why" of it is far too complex to try to simplify into a one-size-fits-all answer. For instance, our own decision making power, delegated to us by God, comes with consequences both good and bad. Choices made by other people also affect our lives. Satan is another force trying to push us down. And God himself is training us to fulfill our destiny. One or all of these forces impact our lives at any given moment. It would be arrogant of me or anyone else to pretend to know exactly what you are going through or to try to fix your pain through the pages of a book. The answer could take many different twists and turns.

Job's friends tried to tell him his suffering was simply because he was a prideful sinner. Jesus warned several times that we should not try to judge a person's innocence based on their circumstances. It was not the sin of an individual that caused suffering in John 9:3. On the other hand, He also told some people that they needed to stop sinning or consequences were going to catch up with them (John 5:14, 8:11, Heb 10:26-27). These things are not contradicting each other; they are just a good example that one-size, blanket statements are not always true.

My biggest obstacle to trusting God in the darkest times was that I, like Job and his friends, had some misconceptions about His character. I had also grossly oversimplified how bad things happen. My misconceptions may not be the same as yours. It is important for you to search out your own places of doubt and find the truth so that you can begin to trust God.

This can be a difficult thing to do. There are many opinions about God and the meaning of His Word. It's my opinion that all of the denominations in Christianity have at least a nugget of truth they've built themselves on. Listening to only one opinion may leave our theology with holes. On the other hand, listening to every opinion may leave our theology confused. I don't pretend that weeding through it all is a quick or easy thing to do. But I can attest that the lifelong pursuit of God is abundantly rewarding! The truth is in God's Word, both the written Bible and the man called Jesus. Pray for wisdom to discern the truth, and never stop pursuing Him.

It is easy to get caught up in the pain and trying to explain its causes. But since God uses the example of parenting to teach us about how and why He does things, I want to take a second and talk about pain from a parent's point of view.

If I could bring my kids to make mature decisions on their own without allowing them to encounter any pain, I would do that; but part of Eve's consequences was that growing to maturity and entering the next phase of life was going to be painful.

I've noticed a growing trend of parents who try to protect their children from all difficulty. This is not always kindness on our part. This approach usually ends up with stunted children who never learn to make wise decisions or have the coping skills to make it through difficulty when we are gone. The resulting fear and indecision are crippling. The inability to make sound choices carries consequences far more painful than anything we would do to them.

There are two kinds of pain parents allow for the benefit of their children. One is active discipline (Eph 6:4, Heb 12:1-12, Rev 3:19, Prov 13:24). As parents, we are obligated to use some form of discipline in order to teach our children self-discipline. It is not supposed to be motivated out of hate or frustration, but to bring them past their selfish, instant gratification into a place of maturity for their own good. God is the greatest Father there is. If He gave us the wisdom to discipline our children, then it cannot be unloving for Him to allow this type of pain in our lives.

The second type of discipline is passive. By allowing the child to experience the consequences of their choice, we give them the opportunity to grow and learn in a hands-on manner. Often it is the only way certain children will learn. It can also be the most lasting lesson. You can tell them a thousand times to get their coat on, but until they go outside and experience the chilling effect for themselves your advice seems too constrictive to be reasonable.

It takes a lot of wisdom as a parent to decide which goal is of the most benefit for our children at the moment, protection or maturity, both are extremely important. It is often heart wrenching to watch them struggle, but if we never let go of their hands, they may never learn to walk on their own. Even if we wanted, we cannot protect them from all pain. That's not how this broken world works. Allowing them to fall down in a controlled environment under our watchful eye is sometimes the greatest love and support we can offer them. It is far better than letting them experience the pain later in life without us to love and comfort them. This is exactly what it looks like when we read about God watching over his children with open arms to comfort us. The goal is maturity, not simply causing pain.

There's another reason that pain is not the worst thing we could allow them to experience. Pain, whether physical or spiritual, is meant to warn us of an underlying problem that needs attention. We ignore it to our own peril. There is danger in removing a warning sign when the true need is repentance or forgiveness more than ease. Praying that warning pains will miraculously stop just treats the symptom but does nothing to fix the true cause. If repentance is needed but never occurs, there may be greater consequences to bear than what is going on right now (Matt 12:43-45). We must carefully get to the root of the problem, not just treat the symptom.

Other reasons the Bible gives for allowing troubles are to refine us, to strengthen us, to change our world view, to get us to look beyond ourselves, to grow our faith in God and in ourselves as God's children (see Rom 5, Eph 3, Jas 1, 1 Pet 5:6-11). This is not an exhaustive list by any means. No matter why He permits it, God only allows what will mature us and equip us to govern well whatever He entrusts to our care. God isn't out to destroy us.

Like Job, sometimes God allows "what [you] fear to come upon [you]" to free you from that fear (Job 3:25). It's not an angry lightning bolt from heaven, but because He loves you and hates to see you captive to your fear. Fear is debilitating and keeps us from living life abundantly. Love always wants to see you free from self-destruction. He wants you to live fully free with true joy and peace, knowing your true worth.

Your labor isn't about God bringing you pain to punish you or break your spirit, but your pain can be the pressure that pushes your soul toward the light. Jesus said you must be born again. If you give up now you will have labored in vain. When our birth pains are not given direction and allowed to bear fruit in our lives, the hurt and frustration they cause our soul only compounds and the opportunity to grow stronger is lost (see Isa 26:18).

No matter the situation you are battling, this is not the end of your life; the labor pains will end. The scars of change might be permanent, but the intense, overwhelming pain can fade and heal. Even if your current prognosis is terminal, your story will go on into eternity. The testimony of integrity and hope you leave behind may change the world. This pain can be the very catalyst which births the abundant freedom your soul has always longed for. For this to happen we must allow God to direct the painful pressures of life.

Peace comes from trusting the character of God to love us and push us to be the best version of ourselves possible. Being in control is a natural human desire, but it is not an option in this broken world. Instead, turmoil is a new opportunity to grow and learn. After years of walking with God and getting to know His love, there are sometimes even thrills in riding the waves of life together. The birth-pains of life can be the very thing that produces our heart's desire if we allow them to do their work in us.

# Chapter 7

## The Wild Donkey

"Who sent out the wild donkey free? And who loosed the bonds of the swift donkey?" (Job 39:5, NASB)

The wild goat illustrated that God watches us benevolently, not like a lion ready to pounce. With the example of the wild donkey God tackles the dark zone that Job and his friends were unable to discuss civilly with each other. That is, if God sees it all, then why doesn't He do something about those guys over there who are living it up, breaking all the rules, and enjoying their life until it's over? Why are they free to do whatever they want? Isn't it God's job to control them?

God began answering just such questions by asking His own:

"Who let the swift donkey go free?"

No one, it was born wild.

"Who untied the feral donkey's ropes?"

No one, it escaped. The Hebrew word used here for "feral" means "fugitive or to sequester one's self." It implies choosing one's own destiny as a willful act of running away to be alone.

Many theologies say that before creation began, God preordained everything that happens. We are simply living out the prewritten script. Job seemed to believe this too (Job 7:1-10). Their logic focuses on the word "predestined." The Greek word is "*proorizo*." If you take the word apart, it literally means "previously established boundaries (horizons)." Before creating anything, God established the boundaries of the story. This includes both the wide horizons of possibility and the bull's eye of what is perfect—and everything in between. Each possibility has a pre-established consequence.

The word for "sin" (*hamartia* in Greek) means "to miss the mark, or the bull's eye." Sin is simply living outside the boundaries God drew to define perfection. Perfection is looking exactly like Him.

Yes, God knew we would miss the bull's eye of His plan, but He did not make that choice for us. Instead, the choice between good or evil is well within the horizons of possibility. We are not simply living out a scripted life where all the choices were determined before the world began. For all of humanity, life in the wilderness is a choice, not a foregone conclusion for some and not others. Many people have become feral as a willful act of rebellion, just like the second type of donkey. It is a sin, but not a surprise to the plan of God.

> "Who put in place its desert home and the salt flats for its habitat?"

God did.

> "It mocks the bustle of civilization and completely ignores the taskmaster's shouts; instead it ranges the hills for pasture and searches for anything green."

There are two types of wild donkey spoken of here: those who were born in the wilderness and those who ran away from their masters. Both have lessons to teach us and hope to offer. Job would have instantly compared them to his 500 well trained animals the Sabeans had stolen from him. It is this comparison that will teach us the most about what God is trying to convey.

The wild donkey Job would probably have known was something like the Asian Wild Ass. It used to roam the Arabian Peninsula, Russia, China, Mongolia, and India. The Persian Onager is the sub-species still found in Job's vicinity. The onager, as the fastest known wild equine, has the moniker the "swift donkey." It is one of the few species of truly wild equine in the world today. It has never been tamed since the species branched off from other equine. It is *not* the ancestor of the domestic donkey. Why? Because of its stubborn refusal to be broken. It is, and has always been, wild.

Compared to Job's sophisticated work animals, these wild beasts were good for nothing, hogging precious resources and giving nothing in return. Even worse to him would have been the lazy runaways who knew the right thing to do but shirked their responsibility in order to seek their fortune in the wild. Both were the antithesis of what Job considered honorable character. If any one of God's creatures was worthy of a good hailstone from the storehouses of wrath, these rebellious asses were it.

Once again, that was not God's response. God didn't actively put these donkeys out of the fold. He did not pre-write their story and cast them as the rebellious ones. They left as a willful act of defiance toward God's plan to make mankind their caregiver (Gen 1:26). Yet did God destroy them for this act of disobedience? No. He gave them a habitat in which to find their own way.

When I first read God's provision of the "salt flats," I thought of salt marshes. However, that luxury is far from what the wild donkey endures. The soil is barren and dry. Few plants can endure the saltiness. Imagine the terrain around the Dead Sea which was just northwest of Job's city of Bozrah. It's an extremely difficult place to eke out a living. This wild donkey must truly "explore the mountains for his pasture and search after every green thing." It's a hard existence--always looking for the next meal. It must range widely for food.

It could have joined the other equine under the care of man. It could have been provided for even in hard times, but it sneered at that option and chose the salt flats instead. A hard life searching for fullness wasn't God's plan. Instead, it's an alternative provision for the rebellious.

Somehow Satan makes the hard life in the wilderness seem sexy. The wild jack-donkey lives the life most would call freedom. Instead of forming a tight knit family herd with a strong stallion at the head, male onagers tend to stake out territory at watering holes where they know the female herds will have to visit. The dominant jack earns the right to live it up with any jenny that passes by. It can go anywhere and do anything it wants with no one to boss it around. It eats. It roams. It scratches. It's not tied down to a family. It's fast and strong and fierce. It has no responsibility. Try to tame it, and it will kick you in the face. When startled, it doesn't wait to find out if you are friend or foe before running away or trying to kill you. It survives on its talent and wit. There are no rules, only live or die.

"He scorns the tumult of the city. The shouting of the driver he does not hear" (NASB). Donkeys that choose to live in civilization are just a noisy bunch of ninnies who break their backs to serve the man. Suckers! Sounds a lot like how the secular world views followers of God, doesn't it? It might even be easy to believe it until you take a closer look and compare what the two lifestyles really have to offer: Peace and purpose in a relationship with the Creator, or fear and survival of the fittest without Him.

Job didn't feel he had such a choice. He felt like he was a slave living out preordained days. God was a shouting driver forcing him down the furrow of his life. Was this true? Could it be that he had a choice as well? Just like the donkey, Job did have a choice. God is looking for voluntary loyalty born out of love and respect, not coerced slavery on any terms.

We can learn a lot about voluntary cooperation by comparing the wild donkey with the domesticated variety. As Job well knew, both domestic and wild donkeys are as stubborn as...well, donkeys. But there is one main difference between the two which leads to the choice of obedience or disobedience. The most primitive difference can be summed up as curiosity.

When a Persian Onager perceives a threat it acts immediately on reflex before finding out if there is any real danger. It jumps at shadows and runs from nothing. It will stomp a friend to dust in surprise.

On the other hand domestic donkeys have a time delay. This trait is shared with what is thought to be the ancestor or close relative of domestic donkeys, the African Wild Ass. Unlike its rebellious Asian counterpart, the *Equus Africanus* is inquisitive. When the African Wild Ass perceives a threat, it freezes motion and then investigates before deciding what to do. It will either decide there is no threat and go about its business; or if a threat is perceived, it will fight like crazy trying to stomp the offender into the ground.

Humans are a lot the same. We either react to our fight or flight response immediately, or we delay reaction long enough to make a better decision.

In order to overcome our initial response to run from God or to fight Him, we must first inquire about His true nature. We must decide if He is there to harm us or help us. Is He truly a lion waiting to devour us, or is He a lamb willing to give Himself to the lion so that we can escape?

Our ability to trust Him is based on our assumptions, some of which we may not even realize we have. It is human nature to assume we have enough information to make a good decision. If the decisions you have made up until now have led you around a barren wilderness of fear and doubt, it may be time to stop and investigate the character of God a little further. Is He the hard taskmaster you always assumed, ready to whip you at any moment, or is He the loving Father of the universe? This is something you have to decide for yourself before you can let down your guard and trust Him.

God knows our need for answers. That is why even with all of Job's questioning he "did not sin" (Job 1:22). We should question and grow. It is important not to search for proofs of our assumptions, but to ask God with an open heart for the truth. Our Father doesn't mind when we ask questions. He is a patient teacher. Many of the Prophets were full of all sorts of questions toward God. The Book of Habakkuk is all about questioning the motives of God, and he wasn't the only prophet to directly challenge God's intent. Our relationship with God is about loving each other. How can we love Him without knowing Him? How can we know each other without asking questions? Questioning isn't necessarily rebellion. Choosing to disobey with or without all the facts is rebellion.

We have the choice to live in God's green pastures or in the salt flats of the wilderness. It is up to us to determine which life we want. We tend to be conflicted. We love the idea of a Caregiver but hate His system for running His Kingdom. We just want to love ourselves and not have to do all the work involved as citizens of the Kingdom of God. What we don't realize is the things He is trying to teach us are for our greatest good, to bring about our destiny as princes and princesses over this world (Gen 1:28).

If we abdicate our position under Him in lieu of the wilderness, we do not gain the ability to rule the world anyway we want. We merely gain the need to fight for what should already be ours. Our scope of influence shrinks to only those we can dominate, and barely lasts for as long as we can pull it off.

In order to determine what we really want we must look at what life is really like in the wilderness. Is this form of freedom our heart's desire? While not being tied down to responsibility might seem glamorous, it will not satisfy our heart's desire the way we would expect.

The wild donkey must scrounge for sustenance often making due with low quality fodder. It's always afraid. It is ready to run or fight at any moment. If it's not the fastest and the strongest, it might get eaten. It's never safe. It can never let its guard down. It must always be on, always wary. One dry spell, and it's in danger of starvation. A moment of weakness, and it's someone's lunch or new pants. If you're not the dominant jack, you get nothing. Everyone is vying to be dominant. Even if you are the dominant jack, you must always search to satisfy yourself. Your god is your stomach (Phil. 3:19). You live to consume. There is little time to devote yourself to a higher purpose. Joys are short-lived. It is life on the salt flats. It is the alternative to life abundantly.

Job and his friends observed the hard knocks endured by people living outside of God's ways. They interpreted these hardships as punishment directly from a god who orchestrates every moment. They didn't see it as merely the result of choosing to live in the wilderness outside the boundaries God set up.

When we choose a relationship with God, He becomes our intimate caregiver. We no longer have to search for what will satisfy the emptiness in the pit of our stomach. He has already provided and prepared. He knows just what we need and when we will need it. You have the choice to live in the wilderness, or you can come into the fold. God is calling each of us home; will you hear it as a driver's shout or as a shepherd leading you?

We all live in a world where life will have seasons of drought and famine. But when you can trust the Caregiver to lead you through these valleys of death to the Source of Living Water, the impact these experiences have is completely different. Instead of making us feel powerless or hopeless, we can learn from them and be empowered. That can't happen as long as we are trying to maintain control of our lives.

Jesus said it like this:

> No one can serve two masters. Either you will hate the one and love the other, or you will be devoted to the one and despise the other. You cannot serve both God and money. Therefore I tell you, do not worry about your life, what you will eat or drink; or about your body, what you will wear. Is not life more than food, and the body more than clothes? ...So do not worry, saying, 'What shall we eat?' or 'What shall we drink?' or 'What shall we wear?' For the pagans run after all these things, and your heavenly Father knows that you need them. But seek first his kingdom and his righteousness, and all these things will be given to you as well. Therefore do not worry about tomorrow, for

tomorrow will worry about itself. Each day has enough trouble of its own. (Matt 6:24-34, NIV)

He also says, "I am the Bread of Life." "I am the Living Water." "I am the way, the truth, and the life." "Robe yourself with righteousness." So much of the time, we think God should supply stuff to meet our need, not realizing our greatest need in life is to be loved. God is love. He is our source for value, hope, and security. He may or may not supply our need for stuff through that new job we've been praying for. Instead, God will address the true need of our soul—the deeper need—using whatever tactic we may respond to. Life abundantly is more than just food and clothes.

Humans under the care of God don't have to chase value or security. We can trust our faithful God to provide the things we need—even in the dry season. But humans tend to search for that third option. We want to get the luxury of a caretaker without having a boss. We want everything to be easy, but we still want to be out there where we can do as we please—even if it will hurt us. The lush life in the wilderness is a myth; it doesn't exist. In a fallen world, it just doesn't work that way. It is a story advertised by "The Father of Lies" to occupy us and get us to keep looking for alternatives instead of enjoying the life of purpose and provision offered in the fold of God. No one is ever truly without any master at all. He is either a slave to fear and the whims of the wilderness, or he must choose a relationship with the Caregiver.

What is the end result of rejecting a caregiver and choosing to live in the wilderness? Let's compare. For the individual wild donkey it means most die at a younger age than their domestic cousins. For the species as a whole it has lead to the near extinction of the Asian Wild Ass while the domesticated donkey lives all over the world. There are only a few hundred wild donkeys including all the subspecies while the tame donkey is more than 41 million strong and growing.

There are a couple of Proverbs which illustrate this concept. Proverbs 14:12, "There is a way that seems right to a man, but its end is the way to death" (ESV). In fact this one is so important it's in there twice more (see Prov 16:25 and 12:28). We might think that freedom in the wilderness is really living, but it leads to an eternal and often early death. True, abundant life is found only in the fold of God.

Not only might the wilderness kill us, but due to isolated, small populations, the wild donkey is threatened by inbreeding and genetic disorders. In contrast, the number of domestic donkey breeds is multiplying and a broad range of features is flourishing. They are short, tall, woolly, sleek, brown, gray, black, white, striped, spotted, long tail, bob-tail, miniature, mammoth, docile, stubborn, out-going, shy, fast, slow and everything in-between.

Satan tries to convince us that by living life our own way we become unique individuals. However, by doing so, we tend to look like the rest of the herd. Looking the same confuses predators and makes it more difficult to single out a particular victim. The onagers all look alike. People have the same result. We allow peer pressure and bullying to bring us all into a norm that excludes our God given talents and unique gifts. It is a tactic developed for coping with certain fears both in animals and humans. We know that we are created to be unique individuals; it's just too scary to try. We might get eaten or maimed. So we find a herd that will except us and try to blend in. Even the most bizarre herds have a certain look or character type they all try to portray.

The truth is, by following the way God offers, we find real freedom and safety to be our best selves. The accepted norm can range widely. God does not regard us according to the color of our skin, hair, or eyes. In fact, He created that genetic diversity and thinks it is all beautiful. He does not mind if you are a boy or a girl, Jew or gentile, low born or royalty, or any other delineation (Gal 3:28, Col 3:11). To Him we are all humans, treasured and loved.

Each individual's gift is able to fulfill a purpose and add diversity and beauty. There is a woolly donkey for cold climates and a smooth donkey for hot. God made people for different situations and purposes too. Some are social; some are solitary. Some are creative; some follow patterns. Some are intuitive; some are logical. By each filling our own niche, we create a world that holds everyone up. There are no people who are less than. Each is important; each has a purpose and place. We may look very different, but we are all members of the same family, genus, and species.

We are valued for our differences. Paul uses the illustration of a body. He tells us that if we find that we are an ear we should not envy the eye, nor should we judge him for not being an ear like us (1Cor 12:16). We are encouraged to develop the gifts God has given us instead of trying to jack-kick those who are not like us. It is not a world where tolerance means we all must look and think alike. It means we are different, and we are valuable in our difference. Unity is working together for a common goal despite our differences, not requiring everyone to look and think the same way.

Wild donkeys all look the same, and they are all consumed by the same activity. The wild donkey is always looking for his next meal. He must search for "any green thing." He must be obsessed with his physical needs. There is no one to toss him a bale of hay in the overwhelming dry seasons which we are all guaranteed to face in this broken world. Paul told the Philippians what happens to those whose "god is their stomach" and whose "mind is set on earthly things." It leads to destruction. They are slaves to finding the next thing that might sustain them.

By using the wild donkey as an example, God showed Job he had a choice. He could choose a relationship with God among the domestic herd, or he could choose to roam God's wild pastures. Anyone willing to listen to the Caregiver is welcome to train with Him.

If we find our relationship with God is distant and our life feels like a wilderness, we can always return to His green pastures (Ps 23). In returning, we must submit to the Owner of the Universe and the rule of love which governs His kingdom. If we choose to trust God as our Caregiver, we have the opportunity to devote ourselves to a higher purpose than simply filling our belly.

Chapter 8

The Wild Ox

"Will the wild ox consent to serve you, Or will he spend the
night at your manger?" (Job 39:9, ESV)


With the wild donkey God showed Job we have a choice.
God provided an alternative to a life of obedience. In the
example of the wild ox, God continues to build on the idea
that we have a choice. He uses a series of questions with
laser precision to cut away some of Job's misconceptions
about obedience to God. Our obedience isn't about slaving
for God; it is all about working with Him to expand the
Kingdom of God, to create a world of love and plenty.

God could not have picked a better illustration for teaching
Job about the inner workings of the Kingdom of God. Job
was master of 500 yoke of well-trained oxen. That's 1,000
individual animals beyond cattle for other purposes. If you
think about the fact that in the Middle Ages whole villages
often shared a single pair, then a thousand oxen becomes
quite an astonishing number! They symbolized Job's strong
investment savvy and financial prowess. As an expert, Job
knew just what it took to create a good team.

The succession of God's questions isn't random. First, it's
important to note that God used the opening question to
make a correlation between Job's feelings of enslavement to

God and the ox's service to man.  God chose the same word for "serve" as Job used in his complaint about hard service (Job 21:15, 39:9).  With each question Job would have analyzed the difference between the wild ox spoken of by God and his highly trained, hard working oxen.  His conclusions directly parallel what he considered brute humans and those who obeyed God.

After making this important association, God then logically followed all of the steps needed to produce a good working team that was ready and willing to serve.  Again, Job would have associated the oxen's journey into obedience with his own and compared himself with those who rejected submission to God.  God broke down the ox's inclination to serve into progressive steps of trust and obedience to teach Job how He is building trust with His own servants.  Job would have followed the reasoning perfectly, but those of us unfamiliar with training oxen will need to take a deeper look at the message God was conveying.

"Would the wild ox willingly choose to serve you?"

No way!  The wild ox which roamed all over Europe, Asia, and North Africa was known as the aurochs.  Though it finally went extinct in the year 1627, their historical contribution to society was well documented.  Job would have been very familiar with the beast.  It was humongous!  Think of a Spanish fighting bull on steroids.  Thick and strong, with a heavy hump of muscle over its neck and shoulders, it stood between five and six feet high at the shoulder.  Its size and weight were closer to a bison than a cow.

Aurochs were known for their ferocity and aptitude for using their horns which could reach almost a yard long!  The violent brutes were not a species to be messed with—unless you were a gladiator.  Even the cows were known to get into bloody battles over dominance.  Unlike most wild animals

93

with horns, the males didn't just posture and show off. Instead they are known to have engaged in vicious combat to the death over dominance. They were absolutely wild and untamable.

One did not simply walk up to a herd of aurochs and choose one to take home to slave in his fields. They were totally unwilling to do the work. Through his experience in choosing the destiny for his own calves, Job knew that random selection based solely on the will of the master was absurd. Because there was a reason for the choice (there was a harvest that needs to be made), then there was reason used in selecting those who were chosen.

So it is with God and humanity. God does not simply go out and randomly pick who will do His work. He calls all of us to come to Him. He then invests Himself in the willing participants who trust Him enough to answer that call. He takes the time and effort to train us to become more than just wild beasts.

To be chosen by God, Jew or Gentile isn't nearly as important as willingness or unwillingness. Talent and strength to perform great works aren't important either. Each person must be willing to follow instruction and participate in their role for the harvest. Our ministry is a matter of aligning our human will with God's.

"Would it lodge by your crib through the night?"

No, even if Job wanted to take care of the wild ox, the idea of it staying in its corral docilely nibbling hay from a manger was out of the question. They were not interested in what a caregiver had to offer. Instead, it would have consumed vital resources without giving anything in return.

The aurochs may not have been interested, but offering the two items mentioned in this question, lodging and food, is one of the first steps in gaining the trust of a wild creature. God says that He freely offers the same to us. Like pastures for the wild ox, God sets up systems to provide for us regardless of whether we have earned our keep. He does this so that we can know He is kind and will take care of us. Paul talks about this stage of relationship in Acts 14:17. He explained that the rain and crops are gifts from God, not because people earn them, but because God wants to fill us with joy because He is good. In Romans, Paul explains God wants us to understand His kindness so we will stop running away and begin to trust Him (Rom 2:4).

After gaining trust, there is a second phase the manger fulfills. For cattle who decide to accept the food and shelter, the owner then offers more to the relationship, something much more rewarding. Cattle can become a team of oxen. It takes time and effort, but there is care and intimacy available to those who join in the work that cannot be had out grazing in the field. Job's oxen would have been brought into the house at night and been fed the best feed by their teamsters, something unavailable to the grazers.

During training, the manger would become something more than a kindness. Every training session would have ended with the very manger that gained the animal's trust. Not only would there be sustenance, but also a reward like grain, clover, or alfalfa hay for a job well done. The manger became part of training, motivating the animal to want to obey its caregiver.

Job was working like crazy to earn these same type provisions and rewards from Almighty God, but he didn't see the rest of the picture. Job's position as master of five-hundred yoke of oxen would have given him a different perspective on this.

There was a third phase for the manger. The idea that the master was there simply to punish or reward would seem preposterous. By the time oxen began pulling a load, the hay and shelter offered by the owner was more than a training exercise. The owner actually wanted what's best for his team and wanted them at their peak. The oxen were given supper whether they had worked that day or whether it was the middle of a snowstorm and nothing was able to be accomplished. A full manger was no longer about enticing results, but about care and respect (Matt 6:33, Luke 12:31).

Like Job, our perspective of God's kindness is often stuck in the reward stage of understanding. Many religions bring their followers to the point of obeying God by promising reward, but then seek to control their followers by keeping them in this immature attitude toward God. God is so much more than just a manger during famine. Our relationship can be based on something more fulfilling than that. We need to mature through the next stages.

The next question God asked contrasted the wooing of an animal with rewards like a manger or shelter and asked if Job could force a wild ox to do his will by strapping it down with a harness. Can punishment and force accomplish what kindness cannot?

"Can you hold it to the furrow with a harness?"

No, Job couldn't force a powerful wild ox to do anything. For one thing, it does no good to punish a wild creature; it will only frighten it further. They are not expected to accomplish any work. Expectation and discipline are for those already in a relationship (Prov 3:12, Heb 12:6).

The harness Job would have used was a wooden beam called a yoke with all its straps and tethers. The yoke holds the team together ensuring that the two move in the same direction, at the same rate, and no one carries the bulk of the burden alone.  An aurochs wouldn't have stood for wearing a harness, nor would it have followed directions down a furrow because it takes a certain level of cooperation between the teamster and the animal to accomplish anything productive.

Just as the manger has different roles to play depending on our stage of maturity, so does the harness.  The first step in training a calf to pull a load is to simply put the harness on it so that it gets used to the idea of being touched and not always going its own way.

As a slave of God, Job viewed the harness as something cruel forcing him down the furrow of life without any options (Job 7:1-3).  Most children view the rules enforced by their parents the same way.  They can't see the big picture.  Yet with a little more information, we can come to appreciate the Laws God established without feeling constrained by them or like we can follow them just right in order to manipulate God into giving us what we want.

First, the harness allows the teamster to direct the team when the team does not know where to go.  We also can rely on the Law to show us how to love when we do not know the best thing to do.  It helps alleviate our confusion and more clearly defines God's instruction.  We cannot always envision what God is doing; but if we can trust God's commands, we will reap the benefit of a bountiful harvest.

Secondly, the harness does more than just enforce the master's command.  It is strapped to the ox to enable it to do the work it needs to do.  The harness is the connection between the ox's muscle power and the load.  Without the straps the oxen have no way to exert the force needed to change the world around them. Without the harness they can scratch the ground with their hooves, or keep the grass mowed and fertilized, but that's about the extent of their effect. They could never help store up for the future.

Likewise, God gives us one command that will allow us to transfer the power He endows in us to the world around us: Love. It is the greatest command and sums up all the others (Matt 22:38-40, Rom 13:9, Gal 5:14). Job viewed the Law as a controlling restraint. It is intended to empower us to fulfill our destiny.

If we see the Law of Love as something we need to escape, we won't be any better off than a wild ox. Jesus said He came to fulfill the Law, not to abolish it; He came to give it purpose, not do away with it (Matt 5:17). Love builds on the foundation of the Law and then raises the bar (Matt 5:18-48). Under grace, we can graduate from practicing rote forms wearing annoying straps which hold us back from having any fun and finally become empowered individuals fulfilling our destiny. The Law becomes more than just a set of rules; it's a tool to help us accomplish our goal. We can grow from unruly calves to productive oxen, and bring civilization to the wild places as God commissioned us to do in the beginning (Gen 1:28).

In Jewish culture a rabbi's teaching is called a yoke. We enter the yoke of Jesus' teaching by believing His teaching is true. Belief enables us to be willing to submit our will to Him and work side by side to accomplish His goal. He calls all of us who are weary and burdened to yoke with him (Matt 11:28-30). Unlike religion, when we are willing to join Him to do the work, His yoke feels light and easy.

If we commit to taking on Jesus' yoke, we are capable of accomplishing great things—not because we are strong by ourselves, not because we know exactly what to do, but because we have joined ourselves to the One who is orchestrating the harvest. In faith, two independent forces are yoked together into one working unit; one cannot move without the other. Every step is taken in sync. The Holy Spirit can then begin to direct us as a team; He tells us where and how to tend others. In this utter dependency on Him for wisdom and strength, we will find unimaginable personal intimacy with God rather than just systems set up for our care.

In order to pick up this new burden for others, we must lay down all other burdens. That may mean laying down our guilt and picking up God's affection for us. It may mean laying down our hatred for others so that we can take up His service to them. It may mean giving up our worries for a comfortable life and taking on a willingness to sacrifice it all.

"Will it till the valleys dragging a plow behind?"

No, the wild ox did not fulfill its purpose. It had the hulk to plow circles around Job's domestic oxen, but it wasn't civilized enough to participate in producing anything.

In order for the harness to produce an effect, it needs to be hooked up to the right tool. A plow turns the dirt to prepare the soil for planting seed. In caring for the world as God's ambassadors, one of the greatest human endeavors is to do the same. The plow is like our ministry to others. We are to testify about the character of God by yoking with Christ to care for the hearts of other people, helping their soul to be soft, and fertile, and ready to receive the seed of the gospel (see Luke 8:4-15 about hearts and soil). The goal of our plowing is to bring in a bountiful harvest, not simply to wear pretty straps and walk in perfect form in order to earn food and shelter from the Master.

Job felt he had been working hard his whole life to fulfill everything God demanded of humankind. He was generous to the poor, just to the downtrodden, and made every sacrifice—required or not. He was plowing perfectly straight rows according to the Law. It was hard work pulling such a heavy load, and he felt that he deserved rewards for his labor. He felt like a victim when life didn't go the way he expected.

It was hard because he didn't have a vested interest in the work. Neither was he yoked in a trusting relationship with God where he shared the joys of His labor. He was still in training under the Law working for rewards. He did not yet understand the point of the work; he only felt the pinch of the straps and the drag of the plow. There is more to it than God demanding we work, work, work all the time.

First, we were meant to partner together with God, creating a world of unity and plenty. Walking and waiting with God is where we will thrive, free of everything that holds us back from Love. Sometimes that means doing something productive together, and sometimes that means a time of relaxation and refreshment. Oxen do not work all the time without rest. Each day they work for a few hours, spend time being groomed and fed, and then they go to sleep and wait for the next opportunity to be with the teamster. There are seasons of intense labor and seasons of waiting. God doesn't call us to serve because He needs slaves. He wants us to thrive! Therefore, He is not only preparing us to love and serve others, but also to have rest in His care. If we walk *with* Him instead of *for* Him, we will never be over-worked or under-worked.

Secondly, the work is primarily about having an intimate, side-by-side, trusting relationship. The best relationships have a common interest, a common goal, a common desire. When we are yoked with Christ in caring for others, we are sharing in His deepest passion. It gives us opportunity to walk together and invest in each other. This produces a deep love and commitment in our relationship. The point is not in the number of sheaves we bring to the barn; the work itself is actually secondary to building a relationship with God.

Thirdly, when our needs are fulfilled in a relationship with God, we don't need to require anything in return from those we tend. Many times in religious settings, ministry carries the burden of producing our self-worth and safety. We do good works to feel good about ourselves. This is not the case when yoked with Christ. With Him all of our needs are supplied by the Lord of the Harvest which frees our other relationships from burdens they could never carry. We no longer minister in order to receive produce from the soil of others. Their approval does not determine our worth. Instead, we minister as a product of our relationship with God, and He supplies our needs freely and generously.

"Will you trust it because of its great strength?"

No matter how strong and well equipped, the aurochs cannot be trusted. In order for the ox and the owner to work together to accomplish the goal, the ox must trust the owner, and the owner must trust the ox. Likewise, our ability to work is not why God calls certain people to a task; it is His ability to trust us that makes the difference.

For oxen there is a progressive journey into a relationship with their teamster. First, the owner takes steps to gain the ox's trust through provision and kindness; the ox must give him a chance. Then the owner begins to teach him by putting on the halter; the ox must acquiesce. As the ox matures, and builds strength, and trust, then the owner may add the weight of the plow. In this stage, the ox will do best if he listens to the teamster and trusts the owner enough to guide him. When their relationship has matured they both are able to enjoy the time they spend together and the thrill of a bountiful harvest. Each step takes trust and participation both from the ox and from the teamster.

So it is with us and God. As we become more trustworthy, God entrusts us with more of our destiny. Each step in our growth toward maturity takes trust in God. The relationship becomes deeper and more satisfying the more we trust Him.

Job was living a life of trying to accomplish the will of the Lord of the Harvest without a trusting relationship with the Lord. He didn't trust God; he was merely afraid of Him. He was being driven down the furrow of life by a cruel master. God's question strikes at the core of Job's belief system. God does not want slaves He wants heirs.

If God wanted to force the wild ox into labor, He could do that. There would have been no such thing as an aurochs. However, we would have been left without a valuable resource. The fact that there are wild creatures which are clearly living contrary to how God created them is an indication that force is not God's method of supreme authority. If it were, then God is a failure. Instead, the wild ox fills another role; it demonstrates God's merciful nature toward the rebellious. God provided pastures for it anyway, with no strings attached.

Even though there are rebellious creatures in the world, all hope is not lost. God will continue working with those who volunteer for the position of yokefellow. He will bring about

His plan with the remnant who believe. He wants to work with those who want to do the work in order to produce the best possible outcome. For those who do not, He has provided the wilderness as an alternative until the end of the age when all will be set right.

"Will you leave it to do the heavy work alone?"

No, that's a ridiculous question. Job wouldn't even leave his best team of oxen to work without a teamster's guide. Just as Job's oxen were not left alone, neither does God leave us alone in the daunting task of caring for this world.

This question demonstrates just how ludicrous it is for us to think God simply lays down the Law and then steps away expecting us to bring His kingdom on earth without Him. God does not leave us alone to accomplish His will by our power and determination no matter how well equipped He made us. Instead, He offers to yoke with us and guide us through His Holy Spirit in a one-on-one relationship.

"Do you believe it will bring your grain back to your threshing floor and then remove it to the barns?"

No, the wild ox benefited no one. It wouldn't even help store up grain for its own winter usage. It had no desire to follow the will of the lord of the harvest because it had no relationship with him and could not envision the benefits of working to store up for later.

In church circles, we talk so often about "believing" that sometimes we forget to really think about what it means. Believing in someone isn't just simply knowing they exist or even knowing some facts about them. Believing takes that knowledge one step further; we're talking about trusting someone's character to do the right thing. This trust becomes a foundation on which we can base our relationship and our choice of actions within that relationship. Job would not choose to ask a wild ox to bring in his harvest because he did not trust that it would be willing to do the work. In other words Job did not *believe* in the wild ox, nor did the wild ox believe in people enough to follow our leadership.

Unlike Job and the wild ox, God often believes in us a whole lot more than we believe in ourselves. He is willing to trust us with more than what we think we're capable of, and that is why He stretches us. He takes risks by trusting us with gifts and talents and things even though we often fail Him by using them to advance ourselves instead of doing the kingdom work they were intended for. (If you want to take it a step farther, look at the parable of the servants and the minas in Luke 19. I'm sure it is not a coincidence that the master entrusted the most faithful servant with 5 coins and the unfaithful servant with only a little to start with. The master knew whom to trust because he was familiar with his servants. The servant's actions were in direct correlation to what they believed about the master's character as well. Their assignment was only a testing ground for a greater role in the master's kingdom.)

Our inability to follow the teaching of God is almost always directly linked to an area of disbelief. The belief system in which we put our faith is inseparable from the choices we put into action. We will do what we believe, not what we know. The wild ox did not trust or believe in humanity; therefore it did not obey. Job did not believe in the aurochs; therefore he did not call it to work for him. If we do not truly believe that Love is the way, the truth, and the life, we will always be searching for other ways to satisfy ourselves. Unless we believe God has the will to do what is best in this world, trying to trust Him will always have our mind and our heart at war with each other, fighting for our security and happiness.

Without trust in God we will always find ourselves pushing and shoving to get ahead in the wilderness. What do you believe about the character of God? Your beliefs will define your relationship with Him and your resulting actions.

Outside of a relationship with God, life is a bloody battle for dominance. Most never get to the top. The fear of no longer being king-of-the-mountain drives us to do irrational things. The battle leaves us with scars and sometimes mortal wounds. Those who don't ever become dominant are left feeling inferior and unfulfilled. Life is less a fight for dominance and more one of survival. It's a matter of scrounging enough to get by on while the dominant try to hoard all the resources for themselves. Job described all of this perfectly in Job 24.

For us, there is a possibility for more. If we decide to give God a chance and enter the relationship He offers us, we have the opportunity to find purpose to our lives beyond domination of the herd or scrounging to fill our bellies. Relationship with God results in all the things we crave and want as a hand out. Love, joy, and peace are the product of a trusting relationship with God and cannot be bought, sold, or given. They become a state of being within our hearts. They are not found wearing the harness of the Law or by grazing freely in the wilderness. Both the Law and the wilderness will leave us feeling empty and jaded. Our true value, lasting happiness, and assurance of the future are only possessed in returning to what we were originally created to be—yoked in partnership with Christ to care for the world around us, His Spirit living within us to guide us in the will of the Lord of the Harvest (Gal 5:13-26). It's time to move beyond looking for handouts in exchange for good behavior and begin trusting the Father. Only in relationship to Him will we find life abundantly.

Chapter 9

The Ostrich

"The wings of the ostrich flap joyfully, though they cannot compare with the wings and feathers of the stork."

(Job 39:13, NIV)


God's focus moved across the savannah from the wild ox to the ostrich. She's the perfect illustration of God's generosity toward someone Job would have considered worthless trash. Yet God's love for her is personal and irrevocable. To draw this illustration, God compares the ostrich's selfishness to the stork's loving care. The contrast is significant. According to every standard the ostrich fails at the most basic task given to every species—procreation. It can't even love its own offspring enough to put them first. However, the ostrich was not obligated to meet a certain minimum requirement of good behavior before God endowed her with extraordinary talent. She was gifted without regard. Yet even with such fantastic gifts, she may still perish if she does not engage in them.

> "The ostrich rejoices in her beautiful wings, but are they the feathers of a loving bird [stork]? She abandons her eggs on the ground to be warmed by the dirt forgetting that the foot of any living thing nearby may

crush and destroy them. She treats her young harshly and does not waste the effort of concern for them. Because she purposely forgot God's wisdom, understanding was not apportioned to her. Yet when she gets up, she laughs at the trained horse and rider." (Job 39:13-18)

Apparently, the ostrich was regularly used as a proverb for how not to act. Lamentations 4 likens the actions of the people of Israel to the "heartless" ostrich. The Bible often lumps the ostrich into lists with jackals, owls, dragons, and monsters of the desert. Even Job did this (though some versions interpret the word in Job 30:29 as owl, it is the same word used here in Job 39). It was a creature that painted a picture of selfish foolishness.

God wasn't exaggerating the ostrich's poor parenting skills. Let's look at why the ostrich had a reputation for being neglectful and harsh. First, ostriches live in a harem group, one male with several females. To make a nest the male scratches out a shallow depression in the sand by sweeping it aside with his wings. All of the females lay their eggs in this one dent in the ground but, only the male and dominant female incubate the eggs. The other females just leave the two of them to be responsible and go about their merry way, abandoning the care of their young to someone else. Many translations say "She treats her young harshly as if they are not hers." That's because many of them weren't.

Secondly, the dominant female puts her own eggs in the middle of the clutch, chooses a few more, usually about twenty in total, and then kicks the rest out of the nest. The area around the nest can be littered with discarded eggs. The other females do not usually gather them up and try to rescue their own eggs; they just let them die, unprotected and uncared for.

Thirdly, sometimes the parents sit on the eggs, but often they just let the sun and sand keep them warm. The dominant pair stays nearby and keeps watch over the nest, often defending it from major predators like lions, hyenas, jackals, and warthogs. But if the adults get too distracted by foraging, the nest is vulnerable to attack by hungry carnivores or the careless feet of passing herbivores. With all the dangers, less than ten percent of nests hatch. Of that, only about fifteen percent of hatchlings survive to adulthood.

God also implies that the ostrich is vain and proud of her feathers. "She rejoices in her beautiful wings." This is never more apparent than in her interaction with the opposite sex. The courtship performance of ostriches is an impressive dance that displays just how lovely their feathers really are. Both males and females will spread their wings wide and swoop them up and down and wave at each other. They bow and twist, boasting their healthy plumage. The males with the prettiest feathers are chosen first. The females seem to clap their pinions with a shaking motion in approval of the show. For Job, watching the ostrich's courtship dance would have been like a prudish Puritan watching a Twenties flapper shaking her tasseled dress on stage.

Though feathers are useful to ostriches for other things, they are not functional for flying. Through his conversations, we can see that Job put value on usefulness and modesty. For him, the ostrich would have seemed just the opposite, wasting her wings on showing off.

In Job's estimation what can be worse than someone so vain, prideful, and self-absorbed that she was more involved in preening her feathers than in caring for her own babies? She's like the lowest of the morally low. Surely God would not bless such a creature! God should destroy her!

109

In contrast, the word for stork is "*chasidah*." It is related to the word for mercy, kindness, compassion, or piousness. The White Stork is still one of the most prominent species of stork throughout the Eastern Hemisphere. It's known and revered in many cultures for its parental care and hospitality.

Rather than scratch a dent in the dirt, the stork builds an elaborate, towering nest made of sticks and other debris. Its nest can be almost five feet in diameter and up to six and a half feet deep. Storks often build their homes high on roof tops and chimneys or in forests near our settlements. The thrifty bird is known to reuse the same nest year after year.

Storks are wonderful parents. After becoming a strongly bonded pair and providing a suitable home, the couple cares for an average of four hatchlings. It's often seen preening its babies; to humans this would seem like a loving nuzzle. Stork parents have also been known to use little bits of moss to squeeze water into their chicks' beaks for a drink. What a tender picture that draws! At feeding time, it doesn't show preferential treatment by picking the loudest mouth or the largest chick. Meals are divulged into the nest for all to feast upon. Everyone gets their fair share. Unlike other carnivorous chicks of mismatched age and size where fratricide is common, stork siblings do not have to compete with each other for their parents' care and therefore don't try to kill each other. Storks will even care for their offspring for up to twenty days after they have left the nest.

One Spanish study showed that around forty percent of its tagged chicks returned in subsequent years to breed. Contrast that with the ostrich. If they each had 100 nests, the stork would have 160 out of 400 babies survive to build their own nests; the ostrich would only have less than 30 out of 2,000 eggs make it to a year old. The stork's tender care makes a big difference in the future of their kind.

In addition to their parental skills, the stork preys on many vermin we find abhorrent like snakes and frogs, moles and shrews, scorpions and other creepy critters. This makes them welcome in many communities. Due to its beneficial nature, harming this bird has been against the law in many nations for millennia, possibly even as far back as Job's own era in sophisticated cities like Thessaly. They were considered good luck and a good omen.

Also, Storks will allow other birds, including sparrows and starlings, to share a portion of their nest. This allows some protection for the smaller birds. This hosting of other creatures in its home gives it a friendly, hospitable anthropomorphism.

There is no contest as to which bird Job would have given gifts and praise. In Job's mind the stork's value would far exceed the ostrich. It's a mentor and a teacher to humanity. We should strive to be like it, caring and hospitable. Surely God should love and bless it.

Is that the point God makes with these two birds? No! This parable doesn't have the same ending as Aesop would have written for it. God makes a vastly different point to Job. He details everything the ostrich does wrong and then adds a huge "yet" at the end! You think the ostrich is not good enough, yet I bless her with an amazing gift of speed.

God didn't wait for the ostrich to be righteous before He blessed her with talent. He didn't make the ostrich earn her beautiful feathers either. He gave to her generously of His own free will because it is His character to do so. He doesn't withhold from His creation because we are unworthy. We can either accept His gifts or deny them, but we cannot earn what God has already determined to give to us.

And, oh, what a talent He gave her! She is the fastest animal on two legs. She's so fast she could have quickly outpaced the fastest speed Job had ever gone. Even galloping full throttle on a horse, the ostrich could have run right past him! An ostrich can sprint about forty-three miles per hour and easily traverse sixteen feet in a single stride.

The ostrich had little to fear from any hunter astride a horse until the introduction of modern weaponry and the inception of the modern thoroughbred. The ostrich would usually have gotten away from bows, arrows, and spears. God gave her the very talent that allowed her to escape all consequences for her thoughtlessness. God says she would have done it with a, "Nah, nah Boo-boo!" She "scorned" the horse and rider. She would have made a clean escape with her God-given talent and been a sore winner to boot.

I have seen special talents endowed in humans exploited the same way. People think they are better than others because of some knack that they possess. Little do they realize the Source of their talent. Even less often do they acknowledge that Source to others.

Yet it is God which makes all talent possible. He gifted humanity with great abilities in order to equip us to care for the world around us. He does not withhold potential just because He sees that we will twist His gifts for our own benefit. We need that talent when we repent and return to God in order to fulfill our role in His kingdom. Since God desires all mankind to come to repentance, He prepares the right conditions for us to thrive when we do so, including the talents we need in order to fulfill the destiny He planned for us. God's provision isn't just far off with generalized systems of weather and crops; His gifts are also expressed within us in a very personal way. They are written into the very DNA code that makes us human.

Even with all the billions of people who have ever lived, there is no one like you—ever. You can change the world around you with a talent as small as a quick smile; show love and kindness and you can bring peace to chaos. We need to stop being jealous of the gifts we see in others, and do inventory on our own selves. I know you will find something amazing in who you are that can build up the world around you because I know the One who made you (1Cor 1:26-31).

Even those who are too physically weak to tell their own story can have a net positive effect in the world. Because their lives affect so many others who care for them, they can add meaning and strength to the testimony of everyone they touch. Without them the world would be a lesser place. God can use every part of each of our stories to positively impact our lives and the lives of those who hear our witness.

Ostriches are extremely gifted, but do all ostriches escape from every predator? No. There are many things that distract the ostrich from using their God-given talent to protect themselves and their offspring. For instance foraging for food without being aware of an enemy lurking can cause an ostrich to die even though it is perfectly capable of running away or using those powerful legs for defense.

Humanity has the same problem. It is our responsibility to use the talents God gave us to develop our relationship with God and nurture others. God put each one of us in a position to reach out to someone in His name. He hugs the widow and feeds the poor by partnering with us to do so (Deut 24:5-22, Mic 6:8, Jas 1:27). Whether family, friends, subordinates, or strangers, God has entrusted at least one other person into our care today.  We must engage in the gifts and talents He has given us.  Our best life and our best world are manifested when we do.  This is a huge part of experiencing life abundantly.

However, we are often too distracted by life's challenges or comforts to think about engaging in the gifts God has given us.  Like the ostrich mother, we get too distracted by filling our own needs and don't notice the Enemy stalking or the giant pitfall we're about to step into.  Even if we do manage to find our talents and use them, we tend to only employ them for our own benefit but not God's intended purpose for them.  If we, who believe in the power of God's love, would actually engage in loving the world around us regardless of what we get in return, the earth would be a different place.

Because we neglect to use God's gifts to build up the world around us, we see entropy taking over.  Our world crumbles and rots in a way that it was never intended to do.  When we do not engage our gifts the way we should, the people we are meant to protect and care for are threatened by life circumstances and predation by the Enemy.  We should not blame God when we see the truly poor and needy:  He set up a system to care for them, and we are often the breakdown in that system.  It is our failure as humans to rule with love according to God's careful instructions that allows war, hunger, and need.  Instead of taking responsibility, we sit back and wait for Him to swoop in and fix everything.  That misses the point of why we are here.

The blockade between possessing the talent and actually using it to fulfill our destiny is the possession of the wisdom and understanding of God.  Job 39:17 says that the ostrich did not possess these things.  She therefore did not have the ability to love her offspring as she was intended to do.  Humans have the same blockade (Rom1:21-31). Our dead or immature spirit keeps our soul from seeing how to love others the way that they need us to love them.

The good news is that we can be reminded of what true wisdom is: Love God, love others, no strings attached. As we seek God, He will give us the understanding of how to fulfill this calling in our own personal destiny. He has already endowed us with the gifts and talents to pull it off.

The ostrich is proof that God's love is unconditional. Job's assumption that God solely depended on the Law to dispense justice led him to the conclusion that God should bless the obedient and destroy the disobedient. This belief was rocked to the core with God's little word, "yet." The counter weight to the Law is God's innate affection and pity toward His creation. The Prophets repeatedly state that God must restrain his pity and compassion in order for the judgment of sin to fall on sinners (Jer 13:14, Ezek 8:17-18). It takes a lot to tip the scales from mercy to judgment because God's desire is to have mercy (Ezek 18 and 33, Matt 18:27).

When the scales finally do tip, God's heart is inconsolably wrenched. My whole view of the Old Testament God with all His anger and vengeance was turned upside down when I read Isaiah 15-16 for the first time. God's "heart cries out over Moab." And again, "My heart laments over Moab like a harp." Their actions could no longer be passed over for consequences; justice called for action against them. Yet even for those people, God mourned their pain. Moab was not the "chosen people." In fact, they were the descendants of Lot's incestuous relationship with his daughters. The Moabites repeatedly seduced Israel to worship their horrific fertility/war gods. These gods required human-trafficking in their temples and the sacrifice of children by fire in exchange for provision and power.  Still, God was emotionally heartbroken when it came time for them to live out the consequences of their actions.  When I realized this, God's prophetic warnings began to seem less like an angry judge and more like a desperate parent pleading with their child to change before it was too late.  Even when the scales call for judgment, God always unleashes His compassion as soon as it's over (Isa 51:3, Jer 12, Jer 31:20, etc.).

I didn't fully understand this sorrow of God until it came time to teach my own children to make good choices.  Oh, how I long for them to do right without the need for me to intervene!  Yet I do intervene when necessary because I care about their future and know that their current course of action will eventually hurt themselves or others.  If I as a human still love my children while being upset with their destructive choices, how much greater is God's love for His creation even when we sin?  My love for my own children is but a shadow of His.  I'm so thankful that God has placed us in earthly relationships that help us understand Him better.

God's love toward us is not all affection without justice, nor is it Law without mercy.  It is God's careful balance of compassion and holiness that produces true justice.  He loves us both when we are victims and when we are offenders.  He brings perfect, timely justice for victims and is constantly working to set offenders free from their enslavement.

Like the offending ostrich, I was a broken reflection of Love in need of a heart change.  God rocked my world with one little "yet" as well.  God's love came flooding over me while I was undeserving and selfish.

> "For while we were still helpless, at the right time Christ died for the ungodly.  For one will hardly die for a

righteous man; though perhaps for the good man someone would dare even to die. But God demonstrates His own love toward us, in that while we were yet sinners, Christ died for us." (Rom 5:6-7, NASB)

I was a "sinner," and yet Christ died for me, His enemy, so that I could be freed from my masters and reconciled to God. What God is this! What Love is this! He is a God we can *believe* in! He died for His enemies. How can I accept that love and not offer it to my enemies in return? This is how Love changes everything.

Our failure to follow God's way is not the final word on our future. Though sin and distrust have come between us, we do not have to be separated from Him forever. On God's balance of justice, love carries a heavy weight. He does not reject us while there is still hope for our restoration. While we live, God continually pursues a relationship with us. We may not have Job's dramatic experience with a whirlwind, but He's no less passionately steering us toward His offer of salvation.

God desires us. He has made a way to save us from the death that results from a broken relationship with the Source of Life. However, just like an ostrich must engage in God's free and unearned gift of speed in order to be saved from predators, so we have the responsibility to engage in God's free and unearned gift of love in order to be saved from our Enemy. God has done all the work required for salvation, but one partner does not make a relationship. It takes the involvement of both sides to make a peace treaty.

Before God spoke from the storm, Job seemed totally unaware of God's merciful nature. If Job had listened to the whole story of man and not just the Law of Righteousness, then he would have known that there *was* a Mediator available to restore his relationship to God. Man *can* be righteous before God because of a loophole in the Law. God wrote Himself into the equation of justice from the very beginning. He would provide a Savior, Messiah.

This Messiah was promised to humanity at the same time that God pronounced the consequences of Adam and Eve's first sin (Gen. 3:15). One would come to crush the head of Satan and set us free. We think of the Messiah as a Jewish idea, but really He has been for everyone from the start, promised before Abraham was ever born. The inheritance of the Promise by Jacob was not that he and his descendents would have a monopoly on salvation; it was that he would be a part of bringing salvation to the whole world as the ancestor of this Messiah. Though the Jews have a *very* special role in preserving the story and bringing it about, the Gentiles, including Job, were always part of the plan of salvation (Isa 49:6, Acts 13:47-48, Rom 10:9-13, Eph 3:1-6). The Messiah was meant to be a blessing for all nations (Gen 22:18, Gal 3:6-14). That includes Job's tribe of Edomites, the descendants of black-sheep Esau living in the stolen Land of Uz.

Job was used to a one-sided portrayal of justice. In many ways justice was synonymous with the closed fist of judgment and still is. Yet God was revealing that this is only half of true justice. The other side of the balance is mercy and love for the offender. Adding love of the unworthy into the equation for justice would have been a difficult and powerful concept for Job to grasp.

Many of us brought up in religious environments have our own struggle to believe God's lavish love for all the ostriches of this world. We can probably quote verses that say just the opposite. It's true that love is more than niceness, but that does not diminish the important role that kindness has to play in justice. God is Love, every facet of Him. Everything God does is motivated by love because that is the essence of Him (1John 4). The Law and consequences, free gifts and tender mercy, and everything in between are all about God explaining to humanity what Love is like, what He is like. Though God loves us in our wretched state, He is not content to leave us there; if we are willing, He lifts us up, cleans us off, and expects us to act like His children instead of beasts. When love is seen for what it is, we aren't offended by justice or put off by holiness; neither are we afraid that mercy will bring chaos and rebellion. Love inspires a far greater loyalty than fear.

God's answer to Job is very one sided in emphasizing mercy because God's talking to a hyper-vigilant, legalistic, rule-follower. Job already understands the holy nature of God; he's got that down pat. He needs to see the other side of justice. He needs to understand God's love for offenders and not just victims. Teaching the effects of sowing and reaping is reserved for other books of the Bible written to other, less mature audiences. For now, Job must learn that loving the disobedient isn't unjust. God doesn't condone their behavior, and the wilderness in which they choose to live is full of dangers. Even so, God loves and gives good gifts even to vain, selfish sinners like the ostrich.

Chapter 10

The Horse

"And they will come to their senses and escape the devil's trap where they are held captive to do his will."

(2 Tim 2:26, NET)

Continuing their perusal of the plains animals, God shifts from the ostrich outrunning a horse and rider to focus on the horse itself. Arabian stock have a notoriously regal appearance: tail held high, mane flying in the wind, and muscles rippling with every stride. Imagine the scene as their gaze stops on a band of wild horses grazing peacefully alongside the aurochs and ostrich.

In contrast to this image, Job had just experienced raiders from two different tribes who invaded his world stealing his oxen, donkeys, camels, and workers. These bandits on horseback were fresh on Job's mind. Their mounts were something very different than the horse that grazed the savannah. The beautiful horse was twisted into a weapon of war.

God used this contrast between the free horse and the captive to prompt us to ask ourselves some very important questions:

> Did you give the horse its strength or clothe its neck with a flowing mane?

No, Job wasn't in charge of making horses. It was God who created the horse smart, strong, and beautiful. The horse is the symbol of everything powerful and free. It has the disposition for becoming a helpful companion in building the world. He created the horse just as it needed to be to fulfill the role He had planned.

> Do you make it leap like a locust? The majesty of its snort is terrible. It digs ruts as it relishes in its ability to meet the enemy's weapons! It laughs at fear, and is not dismayed, nor does it turn away from facing the sword. It is above the noise of the quiver, the flashing of the spear and javelin. It trembles in rage and swallows up the ground; it cannot stand still at the trumpet sound. At the shofar's blast it says, "Aha!" From far off he catches the scent of battle and thunders to the captain's war cry!" (Job 39:20-25)

Do you make it leap like a locust? Locusts typically symbolize armies of war. Swarms on the march could devastate whole regions. Considering this, yes, man is totally responsible for every terrible action in the rest of the description. We used the warhorse as a tool of tyrannical takeover. The warhorse devours ground at the beck and call of its commander, and it's anxiously waiting to comply.

How did the peaceful plains horse become a creature like that? First, man took the beautiful horse captive, and then totally remodeled it. They were violently stripped of their natural beauty and became a symbol of supremacy and arrogance. Every strike and wound they survived forced them to become stronger and more able to defend their master. Warhorses required training far beyond the typical riding horse. There was a process of completely desensitizing their innate fight or flight response. The sight flashing of swords, the sound clashing metal, and the smell of death would have sent an untrained horse into a frenzied escape. This horse doesn't just tolerate the sounds and smells of battle; they invigorate him!

Job described how he felt about those who are bent on violence and destruction: the Almighty should have brought charges against them (Job 24). Job was confused that they didn't seem to get the dramatic retribution they deserved. Meanwhile, he bore the full brunt of God's wrath for no apparent reason.

Was God unjust?
If God Almighty knows what bad guys will become, why did He create them in the first place?
Wouldn't the world be better off without them?
Shouldn't He just blast them off the face of the earth before they hurt someone?

I believe God is answering these very questions for Job through the metaphor of the warhorse. The warhorse is wicked, but it's that way because it's captive to the will of another. We blame the rider not the horse for their nasty disposition. This one realization had the potential to change everything Job believed about justice.

Like horses, humans were created good, strong, and beautiful (Gen 1:31). The reason there are people invigorated by violence is the same reason some horses are warhorses. We

122

have been taken captive and trained to follow the will of our new master. Who is this master? He's our great Adversary, Satan, King of the Wilderness. He has legions of comrades to help him. They are all God's enemy and ours (Eph 6:12).

In light of human captivity to these masters, we can think differently about the people in our lives who have caused us pain by not carrying out their commission to love.

Is God unjust? God's idea of justice is almost incomprehensibly different than the humanistic version. We hate our enemies—often with what seem to be good reasons. But God teaches us to love our enemies so passionately we would be willing to die to set them free. True justice is wisdom beyond simple empirical logic. Such "logic" belligerently tries to make the complex ways of love seem foolish and weak.

Should God have never created people He knew would become evil? Well, look at the horse. What would have happened if God had looked into the future and decided He would not create the horse simply because *some* horses would love war and power? There would be no civilization as we know it. Camels and cows could not have brought humanity as far as the horse did. They lacked the agility and versatility to bring us from the beginning of history into the Industrial Revolution. God didn't create even one warhorse that loves to kill and win victories in battle. He didn't make the horse to wield power through fear and dominance. Job could have seen this with one glance at the wild horses grazing on the savannah. None of them followed the orders blown by trumpet blasts or fearlessly faced the sound of clashing swords.

Like the horse, humanity was created to be an integral part of bringing about the plan of God. If each of us would stay within the boundaries He designed for us, the world would be a perfect place. Yet we fail to live within these parameters. God did not cause certain people to be bad or to do bad things; He didn't pre-write their story that way. We've been taken captive. Our nature has been corrupted. Our captors put as much effort into training us to follow their behavioral cues as it takes for us to train a warhorse. It starts from the time we are born. People are broken. In our captivity we have been wounded, abused, and systematically reprogrammed to fulfill the will of our masters.

We could wish God had never made people whom He knew would become broken and selfish. However, this would mean He could never have made you or me. God is perfect. In order for us to be one with Him, we must be perfect also. He created us perfectly good. But since the fruit incident, no one has been perfectly good except Jesus, not even you or me (Gen 1:31, Rom 3). Because humanity chose the Tree of the Knowledge of Good and Evil as our source instead of the Spirit of Wisdom, we're all a complex mix of "good and evil" to one extent or another. Our status on the good-and-evil meter is irrelevant; it is all imperfection when compared to God. Purely good people do not exist. If God was limited to making only good people, then you or I could not exist either. The love story between God and humanity would have been over before the second generation of humans was even born. Be glad God wrote a loophole into the Law so that we could be restored to Him, and do not begrudge God's equal love for all broken people. Rejoice at the beauty of His character whether He must forgive you little or much.

Every interaction with a broken person is an opportunity for us to show them the love of God. We both have the potential to grow from the experience.  Therefore, the world would not necessarily be a better place without them.

Shouldn't He at least wipe them out so they can't do any more harm?  Someday God will bring about the perfect world we have all been expecting.  Only at the very end of the story will that be to wipe evil from the face of the earth.  He will destroy the Enemy and those who choose to follow him, but until then this wilderness is a training ground for how to handle the ultimate freedom of His upcoming utopia.  For now, God is working to set the captives free and teaching us to voluntarily make choices according to His Kingdom principles.  By teaching us to love even in difficult circumstances, God is maturing kings and queens that will lovingly serve the corner of paradise that He bequeaths to them (Matt 24:34).  In this world we can see exactly what our poor choices cost everyone, and we have the opportunity to learn how to grow beauty even in the harshest circumstances.  One of the main reasons we are in this world before eternity is for us to choose love because love is never forced.  Without choice there is no such thing as love.

Instead of plotting ways for God to judge our offenders, we need to step into the authority God has offered us over them: love (Rom 12:9-21).  When we have their best interest at heart and allow God to sort out their consequences, we are free to fulfill our destiny.  We can live life abundantly regardless of what they've done or haven't done.  Justice will come when it must, but we as victims are not equipped to judge like God.  As long as we remain victims, our judgment is clouded by pain.  Justice is best left to the One who loves us all.  Let Him bring it about in just the right time, way, and measure.

God knew humanity would fail before He ever created us.  Knowing this, He could choose to create us or not.  Because of His great love and power, He chose to create humanity anyway. Apparently the risk was worth it to Him; the gains outweighed the cost—even if the cost was His own life. Having some humans who would choose to walk with Him was better than having none at all. Just because some humans remain corrupt does not mean God is willing to blot out the rest of the species. Instead, He is working to restore those who are willing to be restored. Those who reject Him still have purpose and value.

The question for us is: How did we become captives in the first place, and how can we be free? In our modern world captivity to an unseen entity like Satan seems like crazy, religious dogma at first. He seems like an invisible troll who lost his power millennia ago. Most people have never talked to him, prayed to him, or made a silly deal for their soul. The idea of being his pony—yanked to and fro at his beck and call—seems preposterous and somewhat offensive.

The first step to spitting out his bit is acknowledging that the spiritual world even exists. We can't see it, so it doesn't seem real. We are told that the only reality is what we can use our five senses to investigate and understand. Society says that in order to be intelligent, we need to ignore what we can't see, and only trust tangible, empirical data.

That reasoning is intended to keep us ignorant of the unseen spiritual forces at play. We all have a part of us that takes place behind the scenes: thoughts that run through our heads, emotional reactions, and even the decisions we make before we act. These are all part of that unseen spiritual realm, and none of them can be empirically understood. In fact, the unseen thoughts and feelings behind our actions are the most real part of who we are, not our empirical measurements like the size of our clothes, the color of our skin,

126

or even our IQ test results.  We all long to be valued for what is on the inside instead of our outer shell.

Many secularists are happy to delve into the unseen realm. They study philosophy and psychology to explore matters of mind and heart.  But they ignore spirituality which is the missing key to understanding all of these unseen forces.  You see, when God made man, He breathed into us the breath of life, our soul.  Our soul was completely whole and had three parts: mind, heart, and spirit.  This bundle of consciousness was housed in a material body made of dirt and chemicals. Originally our soul used input from mind, heart, and spirit to make decisions, and then our physical body acted them out.

The term "mind" we know; it is the logical part of us.  "Heart" we are familiar with; it is associated with our feelings and emotions.  But spirit is where it gets a little iffy.  "Spirit" is an ambiguous term that many think is as fictitious as a fairy with magic dust.  In fact, our spirit is the part of us able to discern the now unseen realm of reality.  The Hebrew word for "spirit" is "ruach."  The verb form of the word means "accept, smell, touch, and to make of quick understanding."  This definition tells us what our spirit does.  It is like a sensory organ for perceiving and understanding the spiritual world.  God is known most clearly in the spiritual realm because He is a spirit without a physical body (Jn. 4:24).  The function of our spirit is to know the Spirit of God (1Cor. 2:6-16).  When humanity sinned our automatic spiritual connection to the Spirit of God was cut off; it died.  Our understanding of Him was darkened just like a man going blind.

Just because our spirits are no longer able to sense it, does that mean the spiritual realm is not there?  Well, just because a blind man cannot see the sun does that mean its warmth does not shine on him?  Because a deaf man cannot hear the music does that mean he cannot feel the drum beat? In fact, Romans 1 gives a litany of ways that spiritually blind and deaf people can perceive the Spirit of God and come to know Him. If we can think and feel, then our conscience can at least dimly perceive the truth of the eternal power and divine nature of God (Rom 1:20). When we believe, our spiritual eyes are brought to life, and we can see what we could not imagine before. Things that used to be only a part of our subconscious move up into our conscious understanding.

When our spirit is dead, it's easy for Satan to trick us without even saying a word. He hides in the darkness where we cannot perceive him. He takes us captive by pimping tangible solutions to intangible, spiritually discerned problems. He peddles things that will temporarily satisfy our heart, mind, and spirit. Yet because of the fleeting nature of the material world, their affect soon wears off. We must keep going back for more until our need grows insatiable. As long as we go back to his world's system for our satisfaction, our enemy owns us. We need soul satisfaction in order to live the abundant life; these poor physical substitutes will never cut it. Our souls long for more than a chemical reaction to external stimuli.

Our hearts need us to feel valued, happy, and secure. Millennia ago Satan offered solutions to these problems. Back then we went to his temple and had sex with his prostitutes, took hallucinogens, sacrificed our children, and did unspeakable acts in exchange for favors, fun, and futures. We were taught to value and accumulate wealth and power. Really the only thing that has changed since then is we can do all of that from the comfort of our living room without the bother of a temple. He's cleaned up the source of these pleasures a little over the years, even institutionalized them. But we are still using the same old wilderness system.

We all find ways of filling our need in one way or another. We've grown up believing these are all normal ways to find satisfaction. They're just a standard part of society now.

The problem is sex, chemicals, and chocolate cake only help until the hormonal response to these stimuli wears off. A big, fat bank account is always in danger of being wiped out. A fancy house or a new job cannot give us happiness or security either. The world doesn't stand still long enough for them to fill our need for long. What's new and shiny is soon dull and disappointing.

Most of these things aren't even "evil" in and of themselves. Chocolate cake is delicious—just because they call it devil's food cake doesn't mean it's naughty to eat once in a while. But if we eat to feel happy, it becomes toxic and changes from a treat to gluttony. Sex is a fantastic activity invented by God himself. But if we use it to boost our power or self-worth, it can hurt us in ways we don't expect.

These placebos are a ruse to keep us from finding the path out of captivity. In the wilderness, we're too busy drawing and redrawing the lines between which placebos are good and which are evil depending on our cultural ideals. Sometimes we stand on the side of strengthening the boundaries. Other times we do our best to erase them. We waffle back and forth between anarchy and tyranny. We're constantly at war about who's right and who's wrong. Who has the right line in the sand? When is good enough ever enough?

In order to be free, we need to grow beyond good and evil. We must mature to the point of choosing between good and best (1Cor. 6:12). Take responsibility and move forward. If we stay focused on good and best, we will continue moving in the right direction, no more two steps toward good, one step toward evil. We can be free of the constant backward slide. This can only happen if our hearts actually believe and feel that God is the only true way to life abundantly. Love Him with all your heart.

Our minds also need things like purpose, accomplishment, and curious satisfaction. God has a plan to fulfill these needs in us. But we often sell ourselves short with fantasy worlds both electronic and paper back. Even in the real world, we chase blue ribbons and a place in history. Most of us don't attain high enough to find a sense of accomplishment for a moment, let alone a lifetime. In this day and age our curiosity is met with information overload; we know much but understand little. We must focus on truth and love Him with all our minds.

Spiritual fakes for empowerment, wisdom, and hope are also available all around us. We need to evaluate how we are plugged into this physical world's systems to fulfill our spiritual needs. What we use to soothe our spiritual needs will determine our entire world view. It is the filter by which we interpret reality. If we think the physical world is all there is, then all we will "believe in" are physical solutions. I know as many religious people stuck in this state as I do secular. Faith isn't about turning our brains off; it is about turning on our whole capacity for understanding. We need a living, breathing Spirit to understand the world in its entirety!

Satan finds our wounds and longings and offers us lies to soothe them. Most often he crowd sources our friends or the media to feed us these lies. He ties our souls to these lies with strings of expectation. For instance, we turn on the TV which tells us a story that a member of the opposite sex can fill our need. We find a compatible partner, and for a little while it works.  But eventually our expectation of that person can no longer be met.  What was shiny happiness fades to exhaustion.  Our need for value is infinite, and they are finite.  We need God sized value—someone willing to die for us in our most ugly brokenness, someone to believe in us even when we're failing.  A person could never fill that chasm.  Partnerships based on expectation are easily broken.  Even many Christian marriages are not joined together by a yoke of trust working toward a common Kingdom goal with the Holy Spirit on the reins.  (See the chapter on the ox for how two forces become one unit.)  Therefore, they're as likely as secular marriages to fall apart or be miserable traps because only wilderness strings of expectation were holding them together in the first place.

Satan isn't doing anything new.  The first example of his placebo tactic is the temptation of Eve.  He played on her longing to fulfill her destiny.  He offered her tangible fruit when she needed spiritual wisdom.  He told her if she ate it she could be like god ruling her own domain by judging good and evil implying if she didn't, she would remain an ignorant slave.  How confusing!  Being like God sounded just like what God wanted for her!  It was a false problem with a false solution.  She was already "like God," made in His very image.  She already had a strategy to take dominion by spreading God's likeness to the earth, not replacing his likeness with her own.  There was a third option: ask God for the wisdom she needed; she didn't need to remain ignorant just because she didn't eat the fruit.  He'd gladly help her fulfill her destiny—it was His heart's desire to do so!

When she swallowed the lie and ate the fruit, she gave Satan power over her.  The thing Satan promised would make us gods was a trap to enslave us to him.  God taught her that if she ate from the Tree of Conscience she would surely die.

Satan told her, "You will not surely die." She believed Satan instead of God and acted on that belief. In this disobedient act Eve submitted herself to the kingdom of this world. She crossed the boundary of relationship with God and found herself in another realm.

Our own personal captivity isn't just Adam and Eve's fault; we continue to make the same basic mistake they did. We attempt to satisfy our legitimate needs outside of a relationship with God. We follow the empty promises of this physical world. It becomes a mental, emotional, and physical addiction. Satan uses this fiat system as a bit in our mouth and controls us like a warhorse. We are at the mercy of our own bodily cravings in an attempt to sooth our spiritual needs. Satan became our sensei master, teaching his wilderness ways the moment we walked out on God. We chose Satan as our sugar-daddy and divorced God as our husband. We obey the culture without realizing it's him behind it all.

> Don't you know that when you offer yourselves to someone as obedient slaves, you are slaves of the one you obey—whether you are slaves to sin, which leads to death, or to obedience, which leads to righteousness? (Rom 6:16, NIV)

We have two options: 1) Be subjects of the Kingdom of God, living in the freedom and authority He gives us to care for the world in His likeness as His image; 2) Be subjects of the kingdom of this world, dying slowly under the tyranny of Satan in his likeness selfishly trying to fight our way to the top of the heap (Rom 8:1-17). These two philosophies are in direct opposition to each other. We can't say we love God and continue to pursue the world's happiness (1 John). Instead we will become an expression of the will of the one we choose to obey.  All Satan needs in order to hold us captive is to get us to stop obeying God; then no matter what it is we do from there, we are part of the wilderness outside God's boundaries. Satan owns us.

The good news is we can be redeemed from our captivity. Our captivity works much like a credit card.  We go to this world's system for satisfaction.  We take what we want, thinking it's free, but it costs a little bit of our life (Rom 6:23). The problem is we have no life except what was given to us by God (Acts 17:25), but it is not our own; it belongs to our Father (1Cor 6:19-20).  We give ourselves to the world in exchange for a momentary feeling and keep having to go back for more.  Eventually, we rack up a tremendous debt paid for by using days and years of a life that did not belong to us.  In so doing, we owe Satan a great debt because we have used his wilderness for satisfaction, and we owe God a great debt because it was His life we gave in exchange for goods.  Satan keeps perfect legal records and eventually calls in the debt.  Our life is in the balance.  Christ stepped in and offered to pay the debt.  He gave His life in exchange for anyone willing to abandon the world.  We must change our minds about using the old self-serving system that got us into debt and believe in God's sacrificial love.  Anyone who repents and believes in Him can have their debt forgiven.  By His death, Christ paid our ransom and bought us back from the masters who held our destiny hostage (1Cor 6:20, Heb. 9:15, 1Pet 1:18-19, Rev 5:9).  The legal accounts Satan used to accuse us were nailed to the cross (Col 2:6-15).  Since Jesus wrote the check to pay our sin account, we don't have to be stuck in that system any more.  Those who ask God for forgiveness are forgiven as freely as the prodigal son, and Satan must erase their debt account.  He cannot hold our sin against us.  We then are set free from the bondage of Satan and reconciled to God.

There are three interconnected shifts that need to be made inside us in order to be free of our need to return to our old habit of using the wilderness to satisfy our souls:

1) We need a new belief that Love was actually telling us the truth all along that He loves us freely without merit and has always had our best interest at heart (John 3:16-17). He wants a relationship with us enough to settle our accounts and save us (Heb 11:6). His teaching is life, and we can trust Him. Go beyond believing just that Christ died, and start "believing in" Love.

2) We must then let our belief in Love totally change our minds on what satisfies our soul. In other words, repent: refuse to shop at Satan's company store for counterfeit value, joy, or peace. Satisfy ourselves in the love of God and the free, extreme value He has placed on us. Then the traps of the gods will have nothing to offer us through rebellion or religion. Ask yourself: do you believe deep down you can be totally satisfied within the bounds of a relationship with God? Do you really believe everything else leads to death (Gen 2:17)? Or are you still pushing the boundaries, attempting to satisfy yourself according to your own agenda, trying to figure out just how far you can go without getting zapped or losing honor in the eyes of man? It is easy to get stuck in spiritual confusion if we believe Jesus died for us, but don't go to the next step and turn our backs on our old way of thinking.

In order to permanently free ourselves from our ties to the masters' fakes, we need to evaluate ourselves and find the current source of what we are using to satisfy hearts' desires. Unplug our need to fulfill those desires from anything other than God, and then re-plug those heartstrings into God's power and affection for us. He needs to be our only source for value, purpose, joy, hope, safety, and empowerment.

Follow your strings of expectation to their source and untie the bond.  As we do this, we can begin to do what is right—not because we have beaten our flesh into submission, but because our hearts desire is no longer satisfied with what this physical world has to offer.  This is true freedom!  What would it be like to feel valuable, happy and at peace no matter what circumstance life holds?  It is possible if we make the effort to search our hearts in league with the Holy Spirit to show us our true motives (Ps 139:23-24, Mark 7:6-22).

> For sin shall no longer be your master, because you are not under the law, but under grace. (Rom 6:14, NIV)

3) Once we truly repent and believe that He really is the way, the truth, and the life, we need to let belief in His exquisite love for us while we did not deserve it sink in.  Daily soak it up, and let it make us a whole person by healing the wounds created when others devalued us.  Allow this love to create affection for God, which in turn results in loving and caring for what He cares about: others (Luke 10:25-37).  When we feel God's unconditional love for us, we can love others freely.

Staying focused on these three things will create a whole new paradigm.  Bondage cannot stand in the face of such love!  Forget trying to strong-arm sin.  Satisfy your heart's desire with the truth of your immeasurable value in God's eyes, and your chains will melt away (John 8:32).  You'll be empowered to rule like never before because He created you for the task and believes in you enough to do whatever it takes to restore you to it.

Genesis 3 through the ending scenes of Revelation is the story of conflict between God and Satan.  They are battling to win our devotion.  In whose kingdom will we invest ourselves? Whose image we will portray as our God: love or tyranny?

Who will we believe about life abundantly and the power of death? Sometimes the battle is overtly stated; sometimes it is portrayed through types and symbols.

Right now we are living in the middle of an epic story between those two kingdoms. We cannot give up on the plot just because the ending looks bleak from down in the pit. Jesus came to set things right. Until the day the Promised One returns, we have the opportunity to choose to step into the relationship He extends toward us and fulfill our destiny. In the end love wins, and evil is eradicated. Which side do you want to be on?

It all boils down to, "Choose for yourselves this day whom you will serve" (Josh 24:15). Empirical knowledge says serve self; wisdom says serving others leads to an even greater satisfaction. We will serve the one we *believe* is telling us the truth about how to find satisfaction. Faith is our willingness to act on our beliefs despite what holds us back. We will ultimately follow our core belief, not just what we know is supposed to be true with our heads. Our actions are declaring our beliefs. They tell the world whether we want a relationship with God, or whether we are going to satisfy ourselves without Him.

It is impossible to be fully satisfied with one foot in the wilderness and one foot in the Kingdom of God. We can't cheat on God and stay in a relationship with Him; we have to pick one husband or the other (Hos 2). God is not interested in an "open relationship." He doesn't force us to love Him, but He won't share us either. He set boundaries not only for our protection but also so that we can choose Him.

We now have a choice to make: We can follow the plan God laid out in Genesis for us to lovingly take dominion of the wilderness with Him in His image, or we can allow the Enemy to use our strength in his bloody battle for dominance. We can be beaten and crushed into the tool he needs, or we can allow God to rescue us from the Enemy's tyranny. We can defect back to the kingdom we were created to be citizens of in the first place. Will you choose to accept God's gift, rejoin the Kingdom of God, and fulfill your destiny; or will you choose to stay in the muck and mire, fighting to be the horse on top with the masters? Find the cause of the corrupt behavior; find the master. Be free. Then unlock the cell for as many others as possible.

# Chapter 11

## The Birds of Prey

The Lord said to Job: "Will the one who contends with the Almighty correct him? Let him who accuses God answer him!" (Job 40:1-2, NIV)

There's one more group of creatures to talk about before the intermission. God brings Job's attention to the birds of prey, hawks and eagles.

> Do you understand how the hawk flies, stretching its wings above the south wind? Does your mouth encourage the eagle to make its nest on high? It dwells on cliffs and lodges in the inaccessible jagged rocks. There it searches for food with eyes that see far away. Its young slurp blood. Where the dead carcasses are, so is it. (Job 39:26-30)

Man has dreamt of flight for as long as we have lain in the grass and stared at the sky. Some of the greatest minds in history have attempted to invent flying crafts and failed. Even after the science of aeronautics recently solved the puzzle, we are still just scratching the surface of this technology. Teams of highly specialized scientists have now come together to build robotic birds that even have bent-wing flight. That's amazing! It makes for a great TED Talk.

138

Now all we have to do to catch up to creation is make it self-replicating, self-healing, self-programming, self-refueling, environmentally positive...

I can't even imagine Job's bewilderment at how the hawks and eagles could fly. Flight was something as high above his head as the inaccessible, jagged rocks. Yet Job noted that even from the heights, these birds could not see or understand the wisdom of God (Job 28:7, 21).

Though understanding flight was far above Job's head, God's understanding is perfect. God knows down to the minutest detail how to gift these amazing creatures. He wrote all the scientific and mathematical laws and then used them to design an amazing biological machine that can fly. He knows the physics of motion and propulsion, the biology of bone structure and density, blood flow, and breathing, the chemistry and engineering of making a feather both light and strong, not to mention optics, the intricacies of how to make a tiny bird eye capable of gathering data on miniscule moving objects like mice from such great distances. Add to that the sciences of weather and thermals and everything else that goes into the flight of a bird. He encoded all of the right information into DNA so that an organism can develop from a single cell into a successful, autonomous entity that can also build a nest, reproduce, and perpetuate the system. Just in this one example of biological engineering, we can see how far above our intellectual capacity God is. With all of our technology, we are still trying to reverse engineer it to varying degrees of success.

If God is able to write the code of all the scientific laws and properties that go into engineering flight and then use them to design a biological machine that can independently operate on intuition alone, then He is surely capable of solving the equation for justice. Job, not so much.

God gave this astounding gift of flight to a creature Job would have thought justice should exterminate. It eats blood and revels in flesh; "where the dead carcasses are, so is it." This wasn't just a general statement about some random bird. Job had just seen them cleaning up the carnage of the recent catastrophes he experienced at the hand of Satan. These birds fought each other over the bodies of his children and servants who had all died. They were "slurping up the blood" of *his* loved ones because there was no one left to bury them. They may still have been circling nearby. Talk about a PTSD trigger! The scream of an eagle flying overhead must have been chilling.

The rage Job would have felt toward these creatures could be easily justified. They not only committed a very personal offense against Job, but also broke some of the most fundamental laws of God. Eating blood and touching anything dead would have been abhorrent to Job. God had told Noah not to eat meat that still had blood in it, and that there would be an account for every drop of blood that's shed, even from animals (Gen 9). Why did God let these creatures live?

The fact that God saw fit to create, care, and provide for a predator who violated the most elementary understanding of right and wrong must have brought Job's reward-and-punishment theology nearly to the breaking point.

Did God know what He was doing when it came to justice? So many innocent lay dead, and those guys riding their warhorses were over there making a profit off of it while these disgusting creatures slurped up the mess.

Evil seems to feed itself and grow. It just doesn't make any sense. Where is the great wisdom of God?

Then Jehovah answered Job and said, "Do you contend with Shaddi, The Almighty? Will the fault-finder correct God? Let's hear what you have to say.

Then Job answered Jehovah and said, "Oh! Would the insignificant reply? I put my hand over my mouth. Once I have spoken, but I had no answers, twice, but I will say no more."

Then Jehovah answered Job from the tempest and said, "Please, put on your pants like a man. I will question you and this will reveal knowledge of me. Would you wickedly annul justice so that you could be righteous? If your strength is like God, sound like thunder. Please, you are adorned with arrogance and pride, so clothe yourself with splendor and majesty. Dispense your wrath and anger; see all the proud abased. See all the proud humbled. Tread all the wicked down. Bury them in the earth together, let them face imprisonment and never be seen again. Then I myself will confess that your right hand can save you." (Job 40:1-14)

God is saying to Job, "Alright, tighten up your big boy pants; we are going to go even deeper. You believe that I bless the righteous and punish the wicked. Yet, you, who find fault in everyone and everything, accuse me of injustice because I don't judge the way you think is right. You would crush those whom I see fit to bless. Your version of justice is all about you justifying yourself. What would it be like if I did it like you—simply crushing the proud and treading on the wicked? You would be crushed right along with those you deem wicked. If you think you can do a better job than me, if you think you have the wisdom, if you think you have the power, then by all means get up on my throne and pass judgment on those you think are wicked. If you feel your way is better than mine, if you feel you should have the power and the right to humiliate the wicked according to your standards, then you, by all your righteous works, can save yourself."

Do you think I should ground the eagle because it slurps blood? Do you think I'm wrong for creating the horse when I knew what mankind would make him into? Do you think I'm wrong for blessing the ostrich with a splendid gift when she doesn't deserve it? Should I force the wild ox to bend to my will? Am I right to provide for the wild donkey even though they are rebellious and do nothing for me in return? Should I not watch over the mountain goat just because her offspring doesn't add to my net worth? Can I let the baby ravens starve to death because their parents feed them dead things? Should I break the teeth of lions because they prey on the weak and dying?

Job obviously did not have a suitable reply. Job thought that because he had followed the law as carefully as possible, he was worthy of justification. He thought because his good far exceeded his bad God should overlook what little bad there was (Job 7:20-21). God said this is pure arrogance on Job's part.

In Job's version of justice the wicked (i.e. anyone not as righteous as himself) are dealt with harshly and swiftly, without mercy, and without regard to their value or purpose in displaying the image of God. God says that this would annul justice altogether. God's justice is true justice because He is unbiased toward the victim or toward the offender. God loves them both, and His justice is geared to benefit them both.

When we are still looking to the Law to define our rewards and punishments, a great deal of life does not make sense. Often the bad guys look like they're winning, and the good guys are always losing. Only God is wise enough to balance the equation of justice. While eagles may not be able to catch a glimpse even from their vantage point (Job 28), God can see it all. The Law is just part of the answer. Only Love has the wisdom for true justice. We can't understand all the ripples or the "butterfly effects" we would cause if we intervened whenever we wanted.

Take the carrion birds for example; Job would have crushed them. According to the Law given through Noah, they deserved it. But in this broken world, the carrion eaters serve an important purpose. What would happen if God did not show mercy to carrion eaters and destroyed them out of existence? Without them the earth, now filled with death, would soon be overrun with decay and disease. In this decaying wilderness a careful balance must be struck between life and death. Until the Kingdom of God is fully realized and creation is made new, we will continue our love/hate relationship with those who keep balance in the wilderness.

Likewise we cannot understand the role others play in this world. We cannot know all of God's reasoning for intervening to spare one life and not another (Isa 57:1). Our scope of understanding the big picture is too small. There are many questions we don't even think to ask.

God says that Job's lack of regard for the wicked was an attempt to justify himself. This caused him to see others with a critical eye. Job didn't point out their faults to encourage them to choose a better way of life, nor were his critiques because he had compassion on their resultant misery. No, he judged them harshly so that he could validate his own superiority and worthiness (see Job 31). Since he was an extreme rule-follower, he thought he was on another level and would be spared from pain. His world could be neat, orderly, and safe without the chaos introduced by rule-breakers. He couldn't wait for God to destroy them and set him free from the mess they made.

While superiority and comfort may seem like the logical conclusion to rule-following at first, it's an outright lie. The Law is a harsh taskmaster. There is always fear that you aren't doing enough. Every comfort brings an underlying feeling of guilt because comfort means you are taking time off from working toward perfection. The inability to reach perfection is the wrench in every legalistic approach to salvation.

Job could not answer God's challenge because the flaw in his logic was staring him straight in the eye: Even as the most righteous man in all of the East, he was unable to justify himself. God is the judge, and His holiness is the standard, not other humans. Though Job was more law-abiding than everyone around him, his self-righteousness was never going to compare to God's perfection. Job needed God to have mercy on his soul just as much as all of the people he deemed unworthy to room with his sheep dogs. Following the Law is not enough to be restored to God's good graces. As long as we are living based on the good-and-evil meter, no amount of perfection can ever make up for past mistakes. It does not matter how faultless we are in the future. Total, God-like perfection has already been lost.

If we choose to be like the old Job and judge others harshly according to the Law, if we offer them no compassion, then we will be judged with the same amount of compassion and mercy (Matt 7:1-5, Luke 6:27-42). Comparing ourselves to others will not put us above them nor put them below us; it will only allow us to deceive ourselves about the true measure of our holiness.

God's justice isn't as simple as skimming the top 10% of humanity for salvation and destroying the rest because holiness isn't attained by performing a certain number of good deeds or by passing a certain number of tests. Salvation isn't something we do. Even in Job's day salvation was only available by a change of heart: repenting of our agenda, believing in God's character to provide redemption, and throwing ourselves on His mercy (2 Chr 7:14, Joel 2:12-14, Jonah, Heb 11, etc).

Our lives are not about a list of rules. Our relationship with God is not about how well we fulfill the Law. Our lives are about so much more than working the system to get what we want. Life is more than even justifying ourselves so that we can go to heaven! They are about relationship with God starting here and now on earth creating an environment for the world around us to thrive. Relationship is what life is all about. Love God; love others.

Job has been challenged by God to re-evaluate the basis of his justification. Right now he is attempting to justify himself. God is revealing to Job a new understanding of His character. That way, Job can start trusting the compassion and mercy of God instead of trusting in his own ability to follow the Law to gain the favor of the Almighty Shaddi.

Chapter 12

Behemoth

"Look at Behemoth, which I made along with you and which feeds on grass like an ox." (Job 40:15, NIV)

Up to this point God has been undoing Job's old assumptions about God's character and Job's obedience. The next two animals will bring Job out of his deconstructed theology into a full understanding about what God truly wants from us and what type of relationship He desires.

God begins this new turn in the conversation by drawing a tight correlation between Job and the animal He is talking about. He establishes that He is the Creator of both man and this beast. As such He is Lord of them both. They are both responsible to obey Him. He is the same type of God with a constant character toward both of them.

But what in the world is the animal He is speaking about? It eats the new growth of wild plants, so, like an ox, it's some type of herbivore. It moves its tail like a cedar tree. It has very strong muscles. The strength in its legs is like bundles of ropes knotted together. Its bones are like tubes of bronze, the most durable metal they knew at the time. Its legs were like rods of iron. It was the greatest animal of its kind.

The elephant is the largest of the land animals alive today. It is an herbivore, but its tail is a tiny, little fly-swatter, nothing like a cedar. Hippos have the same issue. The creature God describes is unable to be trapped or controlled, not some circus side show. Nothing alive today perfectly fits the description. Most likely, it's some sort of an extinct creature we do not see today.

If we look at all the historical possibilities, the description sounds like some sort of sauropod, the family of brachiosaurus and diplodocus. I understand that for many such a suggestion may seem absurd. Most believe that dinosaurs were extinct long before man ever existed. Please, be patient with me. The concept of evolution doesn't exclude belief in God or the Book of Job. Creation versus evolution isn't the focus of this book. There are many theologians that have no problem marrying the two, both scripturally and scientifically. Personally, I believe that the empirical data should be allowed to take us anywhere the evidence leads— including the catastrophe of a global flood—and have no need to mingle evolution into Genesis. Geologist increasingly use catastrophe to explain their findings, and geneticist are finding surprising bottlenecks. I think the Biblical narrative beautifully explains these findings.

There is evidence to support the idea that humans have interacted with live dinosaurs at one time. Prehistoric drawings and etchings of sauropods are found on rock faces in the American West and on pottery and stones in South America. Ancient artwork of other dinosaurs is found in many cultures from Babylon, to China, to the Norse, and others. There are stories from as recently as a few hundred years ago featuring dragons and serpents that could easily be describing all sorts of dinosaurs—herbivores and carnivores, big ones and small ones, on land, sky, and sea. Many of these creatures and events involve famous, reliable witnesses, both scientists and explorers. I won't belabor the idea with all of the examples I found, but I would encourage you to look for answers for yourself with an open mind. Sure, it's possible that much of the myths and legends are merely fiction. But if they are, they seem to be based on something mankind once knew.

I won't insult you by trying to force you to think like me. If you don't like my idea, research and draw your own conclusion on what animal you think fits best. If you can't swallow the idea of Behemoth as a sauropod just think of it as an elephant or some extinct/mythical mammal to make sense of this example.

For our purposes, it matters less what this particular creature actually was and more how God uses it as an allegory. The animal is fairly well described, so we can still see what God is saying if we just follow the meaning. Since God used other creatures Job was familiar with, this creature is probably something Job would have instantly understood, whether sauropod, elephant, or something else. To me, God's instruction for Job to "Look at Behemoth" makes it seem pretty literal, not figurative.

That said, we need an image of the extinct Behemoth to wrap our imaginations around. I think sauropod is the best fit for it. Like Behemoth, sauropods lived in marshy, river or coastal habitats. They were the largest herbivores that ever roamed the earth, the greatest of their kind. They had tails like cedars and enormous bones "like tubes of bronze." They had to be extremely strong to heft their weight from place to place. It would have been logistically impossible to trap or harness it. No cage could contain it.

What is God's commentary on this creature?

"It is the greatest of the ways of God. Yet the Maker can approach it with a sword. For the mountains bring their produce, and all the wild animals make merry there. Under the thorny shade tree it sleeps camouflaged among the branches of the wetland, covered by the shady tree's shadow, surrounded by tall trees near the river. Oh! The violence of the flooding river does not alarm. It trusts, even when the Jordan bursts forth toward its mouth. Its eyes take notice of traps bated to pierce its nose." (Job 40:19-24)

I believe that as an herbivore, this animal represents the ultimate example of those who follow God's ways. God originally created everything to eat plants and live in peace with other species (Gen 1:29-30). There was no death. Yet through sin, the world was corrupted. Choosing an herbivore to compare to a carnivore like the next animal, Leviathan, contrasts the willingly obedient with the extremely disobedient. Instead of comparing the domestic and wild species of the same kind like the ox or donkey, He is comparing two creatures that are utterly free to do whatever they desire. One is the greatest, peaceful herbivore; the other the greatest, violent carnivore. God is showing how He interacts in both scenarios.

Behemoth can go anywhere it wants with no one to stop it. It is the most awesome herbivore ever created, yet it is not as strong, or as big, or as awesome as God. No matter how big it may seem to us, the Maker is greater. Though humans may not be able to capture this beast, its Creator could at any time draw His sword and end its existence or force it into slavery. The Creator is in full authority over Behemoth's existence.

Is the Behemoth afraid of such a thing? No! God can walk up to it armed like an enemy, and Behemoth is confident that

God has no ill intent. Behemoth doesn't obey out of fear, but out of trust.

The passage continues by giving us three bases that give Behemoth good reason to put its confidence in God. The ESV and the NET versions do the best at reflecting the dependant conjunction "ki" that means "for or because." The Maker can approach it with a sword *because* of what comes next.

First of all, it trusts the Maker even with a sword because "the mountains bring their produce." Throughout the Bible, God sites the fact that He provides the circumstances for life to thrive—before we have done anything to earn it—as a primary reason we can begin to trust Him (Acts 14:17, Rom 2:4). From the very beginning God created the earth as the perfect environment for life to flourish and called it very good. Here we live in the Goldilocks Zone, the perfect distance from the sun and moon, with balmy temperatures, flowing water, and plenty of food. Our planet is not too big, not too small. It has just the right amount of gravity, spin, magnetic field, and atmosphere. Even after the devastation caused by the curse of sin and the judgment of the flood, there is enough of creation remaining for life to continue to thrive today. If we are responsible enough to take care of it, it can continue on for generations more. God knew exactly what life needed and provided the perfect conditions for it because it is His nature to engender life. (Now, if only we would learn to share these bountiful resources with each other.)

Behemoth lives a life of provision and peace. The water cycle begins with rain or snow in the mountains and drains into Behemoth's marshy river environment. This produces a lush landscape for the beast to thrive. There is an abundance of fresh leaves to eat and plenty of shelter. Behemoth can rest in the lowlands assured that God knows how to provide the best circumstances for life.

Like the wild donkey and ox, God provides for its needs through a system that Behemoth doesn't even have to participate in. With sunshine and rain Behemoth has plenty. Jesus gives other examples of creation that live in this type of trust: sparrows, lilies of the field, even ravens (Matt 6:25-34, Matt 10, Luke 12, Ps 104). Behemoth does not have to lie, cheat, or steal to get ahead. It does what God created it to do, and trusts God to handle the outcome.

The second reason Behemoth trusts in God is that it believes the testimony of credible witnesses. When God approaches with a sword, "the wild animals continue to make merry there." God put Behemoth in a community of other creatures. These animals don't even stop playing. They were probably herbivores too since herd animals travel together to alert each other about predators. What do wild animals do when a threatening hunter approaches? Run! They surely do not continue to frolic and play. Yet, these creatures didn't even have to stop and think about it. They knew instantly that God was not a threat to them. They trusted His purpose for walking up to them armed. Their testimony soothed fear when God walked up to Behemoth equipped with a blade.

Do you have a diverse herd of friends who can testify about the goodness of God when you are feeling scared and alone, when God's sword seems to be cutting you instead of healing you? If you don't, church is meant to fill that purpose. We as the Church need to focus on encouraging each other in tough times rather than judging each other's pain.

Having his own herds, Job would have known that if the animals were calm and happy without running away or attacking, it was because they had a relationship with the Creator and were not afraid of Him. They knew Him and trusted Him. He was their friend, and they were His. There was no need for them to fear His sword.

God is not a carnivore. He has no need to consume us. He does not raise us to slaughter us for His own benefit. His leadership exemplifies everything He commands of us, loving care for everyone regardless of merit. God's leadership was demonstrated by Jesus who said the greatest in the kingdom doesn't lord over their subjects, but instead is there to serve (Matt 20:24-28, Phil 2). Far from slaughtering us for His benefit, He is willing to give up His life for ours.

God holds all the power and strength it takes to destroy, but He does not just swing it around wildly, threatening and screaming. The old word for this is meekness—power held by someone gentle, kind, and even-tempered. He's not an unarmed sissy, but He uses all of His strength for the good of others, especially those who cannot defend themselves. God was able to open carry at their party, and no one freaked out.

Rather than shiv His enemy, parley is God's first choice every time. He speaks every language of man and beast. For years on end, He has patiently explained the consequences if there is no change from our current course of action. The Law of sin and death will assume authority over us, and Satan will have his way.

Job accused God of malevolently watching and destroying him for no good reason (Job 7, 10, 14, 16). He described God as a trophy hunter stalking prey just to prove He is stronger. Behemoth and its playmates do not view God in any such way. They trust Him and continue their state of peace and joy even if they see God has a sword in His hand. They don't have to stop their game because they know whatever the problem is, God has it handled. Even a sword must be for their good, meant for their protection and freedom.

This can be seen even in the word for "sword" (*chereb*) which can also be translated, "tool." A tool can just as easily be used for good as it can for evil. But because of fear and preconceived views of God, we jump to the conclusion that God's tool is there to kill us. It is really there to sculpt us into something beautiful, to cut away the cancer that is killing us. In fact, the root of this word is "*charab*." Its first use is as the wind that blew the waters away after the flood, the wind that restored the earth, not destroyed it.

The third reason Behemoth is able to trust God is because of His provision of peace. Behemoth's environment is described very specifically. God mentions the "shady tree" twice. Some versions say "lotus plants." This is the ziziphus lotus tree, not the delicate lotus water lily plant. The flowers from the ziziphus are used in several cultures for courting and romance. Their pleasing aroma is said to make people fall in love. The ziziphus has shiny, green leaves and a sweet fruit called jujubes eaten by many people for dessert. It is used by traditional medicine for anxiety and stress conditions and is attributed with sedative properties.

Homer mentions lotus in the "Odyssey" eaten by the "lotus-eaters." Some of Odysseus' men ate lotus fruit. They immediately stopped worrying and obsessing about getting home. Odysseus had to force them back to the journey. Maybe Job ate this fruit to treat his own anxiety and knew first hand why God put Behemoth in the context of this tree.

This is where Behemoth sleeps. It inhales the sweet perfume, eats the anti-anxiety medication, and is covered by its shadow like a protective blanket. God is speaking directly to Job's life of anxiety and fear by contrasting it with this description of peaceful life by the lush River Jordan.

So often we fail to consume what God has provided for our lives that has these very properties. David writes, "How sweet are your words to my taste, sweeter than honey to my mouth!" (Ps 119:103, NIV). God's Word is full of anti-anxiety truths that we can apply to our broken and wounded spirits like salve. It's full of promises of God's love and faithfulness that provide hope and peace far greater than the ziziphus lotus could ever begin to impart. It tells us about God's character and how far He was willing to go to buy us back from the Enemy. But like the fruit of the ziziphus, it must be consumed in order to have any anti-anxiety affect.

> Oh! The violence of the flooding river does not alarm. It trusts, even when the Jordan bursts forth toward its mouth.

Behemoth was exactly the opposite of Job. Job said, "What I feared has come upon me." If everything that Job feared actually happened, he must have been deep in the pit of anxiety before this story started because he suffered much tragedy. In contrast, Behemoth was calm, free, and anxious for nothing. It trusted the hand of God to do what is best.

It followed God's ways. Yet that did not mean its life was without difficulty. This Behemoth lived in a post-flood world just like we do, affected by environmental corruption on every side. Behemoth suffered in a world spoiled by man's choice to sin. Its habitat was chaos compared to the pre-flood paradise that produced giants of its kind. The river on which it depended for life also threatened to violently end its existence.

Trusting God doesn't mean everything is always peace and safety. Yet we don't have to live in anxiety. Even when the Jordan breaks its banks, Behemoth is not afraid.

Imagine a sauropod like brachiosaurus. How deep would the flood have to be to reach its mouth? If the water came up to its mouth, it would seem like the flood of Noah all over again.

Why should Behemoth have such confidence when faced with dire circumstances? Because God promised He would never flood the whole world again. He made that promise not just to certain chosen people, but to all of humanity—and not just to humans but to every creature with breath, including Behemoth (Gen 9). There would always be a place Behemoth could go to escape the flood. There would always be a way to make it through the crisis or a way out of it. Even when approaching imminent death, it is not afraid (Ps 23:4, 1Cor 15:55).

God makes us the same promise, "No trial has overtaken you that is not faced by others. And God is faithful: He will not let you be tried beyond what you are able to bear, but with the trial will also provide a way out so that you may be able to endure it" (1Cor 10:13, NET). The best way out usually involves a new level of trusting Him like getting on the Ark and going through the storm. It's rarely the easy way and often stretches us farther than we ever could have imagined possible. We may feel sea sick along the way, and the world may never be the same again; but we will be stronger, more free, and capable to lead and love. We will have within us the Creator's power to rebuild. The people I've witnessed actually do this are real-life heroes to their families, communities, and beyond. They have biographies that inspire us to do the same.

One way to possess lasting peace even in the deluge is to know the promises of God. What does He say about the matter?

It's very important to seek God and not just a religious factoid on the matter. We must know Him, not just what people say about Him. Then when trouble comes, we can stand confident and unshakeable. We can be sure that even if our worst fear comes true, God will weave it into something beautiful for our lives and for those who see our hope (Ps16, 21, 30, 46, 55, 62 [one of my favorites], 112, 1 Pet 3:14). God is safety for this world even while the Destroyer rages. If life's circumstances seem like they may overwhelm, God can be trusted because He is not out to harm you. His character is loving and compassionate (Jas 5:11). At the right time, He will blow the waters back. I know this first hand, not simply as a theoretical, works-great-on-paper hypothesis.

> And so we know and rely on the love God has for us. God is love. Whoever lives in love lives in God, and God in them. This is how love is made complete among us so that we will have confidence on the day of judgment: In this world we are like Jesus. There is no fear in love. But perfect love drives out fear, because fear has to do with punishment. The one who fears is not made perfect in love. We love because he first loved us. (1John 4:16-19, NIV)

It is not lack of hardship which produces peace that surpasses understanding. It is faith in the character of God to turn all hardships into blessings which soothes our hearts (Rom 8:28, Phil 4:11-12). I'm not talking about blessings like the perfunctory greetings we give each other in churchy circles, or public niceties after a sneeze, or even as a euphemism for lucky. I'm talking about life changing fulfillment and satisfaction, truly blessed (Matt 5). True blessing doesn't gloss over tragedy or explain it away, but rather repurposes it. God's love takes an experience that could have destroyed us and makes it into something that empowers us. Someone who hasn't gone through a trial can never possess the same authority on the matter as someone who has survived and now thrives. Their testimony is a blessing for their own future like David's experience with a lion and a bear before meeting Goliath (1Sam 17:34-37). It is also a blessing for anyone inspired by their story. It is hope in troubled times.

God can use both the good things and the bad to empower us to change the world and move us forward out of fear and hopelessness into a life of freedom and strength. He is the potter that remakes spoiled things into something beautiful (Jer 18). He can even make something from nothing! Because of sin, pain is inevitable as long as we live. This world is full of trouble (Gen 3:14-19, John 16:33, 2 Cor 4:8-9). This will be the state of reality until the earth is melted and remade (2 Pet 3:10-13). Your worst case fear might come upon you (Job 3:25). But that doesn't have to be the last word in your testimony.

Of all of our fears, death most surely will come upon us, somewhere, sometime. Attempting to avoid pain or death hoping for a life of comfort will cause us to make many bad decisions that come back around to bite us. These actions are based on fear. Short term, they might seem shrewd; but long term, they will be misery. We must let go of our idea of safety and accept the power that God has to bring death to life, brokenness to wholeness, ashes to beauty (Isa 61). Even Jesus died. The worst fear that Satan has dangled over our heads for thousands of years happened to Him too (Heb 4:15). Yet even the worst Satan can throw at us, death, isn't the end; it's only one scene somewhere in the middle of our story (Luke 23:43).

We can only find happiness and security if we let go of our old ideals of comfort and perfection. We must repent of our own agenda and embrace God's will. He alone can bring us into our destiny. That's often a messy process. Safety is not the lack of turbulence; it is a trusting relationship with the Creator of the universe to work all things for our benefit. His Spirit in us has the power to overcome anything.

Now let's look at the last bit. Every time I read Job, the last sentence in the Behemoth section caught my attention. It seems to be an odd tag on the end of such a lovely passage about not fearing God.

"Its eyes take notice of traps bated to pierce its nose."

First, it would have been an enemy, not God, trying to trap Behemoth. Piercing an animal's nose has to do with control. You would put a ring in its nose so it would not do certain behaviors, or so you could lead it wherever you wished. Behemoth does not obey God because God has a ring through its nose. Instead, God's relationship with Behemoth is based on trust. Behemoth follows the ways of God because God is good—no ring needed.

In like manner, God does not try to force us into good behavior. We can choose to obey or disobey. He has laid out the choice clearly for us to make. The ultimate freedom is offered when we take responsibility for our choices according to love (1Cor 10:23-33). Live to love others in a relationship with God, and you will reap a life of fulfillment and joy. Live to love self in your own power, and you will reap a life of emptiness and fear. It is your choice.

Secondly, from its high vantage point Behemoth would see a trap a mile away and evade enslavement by the enemy. The whole idea of capturing it is ridiculous. We need to open our eyes to the enemy's traps. Let your perspective start from high above the situation, and use the wisdom of God to detect the traps of the Adversary.

It's almost laughable how similar Satan's tactics are to that of a hunter. He appeals to our basest needs. Think of all the lures used in catching game. They deal with easy sustenance, pleasure, and maintaining power over a territory.

The freedom of God appeals to our higher cognition. Which part of you will rule your life?

Be wise: choose freedom.  Be leery of free lunch, quick pleasure, and promises of power.

Chapter 13

Leviathan

"Can you catch Leviathan with a hook...? Can you make it a
pet like a bird, or give it to your little girls to play with?

(Job 41:1a, 5 NLT)

God has one last animal to discuss with Job. Its name is
Leviathan. It sounds like a creature of legend, dominating
land and sea. It seems like some sort of an amphibious reptile
with extremely thick armor and a bad temper—like a croc,
only humongous and fire breathing. Many can't imagine
that it was ever real, let alone still living concurrently with
people. It sounds like something out of the tales of King
Arthur or the Norse gods. Oddly, you can find stories like it
from every inhabited continent of the world even though the
peoples never met.

Like Behemoth, the identity of Leviathan is hotly debated.
Several kinds of animals have been suggested. Modern
examples such as the crocodile or whale have been
purported. Extinct animals such as Basilosaurus, Mosasaurus,
or Plesiosaurus have also been theorized. All of them are
apex predators. The extinct ones would have been terrible
sea monsters to behold.

Personally, I use an Egyptian Spinosaurus as a model. It is fearsomely cool! Type it into your search engine for some amazing images. Many details of its life fit the description of Leviathan and will help us visualize this last scene.

It was the largest predator ever to walk the earth (the greatest of its kind you might say). It was fifty to sixty feet long, and as tall as three grown men stacked on top of each other. Just the giant spines on its back were 6-7 feet tall making a sail that stuck up out of the water. If it was anything like its cousin, Carnotaurus, its hide was protected by an array of boney scutes like a crocodile. Like Behemoth, its habitat was in and near the river. It was semi-aquatic and probably lived a lot like a croc, taking advantage of whatever opportunities came along. It would have definitely left people cowering in fear.

Whether it is the right creature or not, Spinosaurus gives us something to wrap our brains around as we dissect the example of Leviathan. Thankfully God gives us a very detailed picture of Leviathan. It is as if God knew this species would go extinct, and we would need all that information. Like Behemoth, whether you believe it is real or mythical isn't as important as following the illustration God gives through its imagery. If you don't agree with my speculation about Leviathan and Spinosaurus, just draw your own image of the creature you think God was using for an illustration.

As for the scientific possibility of fire breathing, I do not have all the answers. Finding their bones does not give us all the information about soft tissues and fluids. There is a lot we still don't know. Yet it is not outside the realm of possibility. For example, the Bombardier Beetle shoots boiling chemicals with great precision at its enemies. Extinct reptiles could easily have had modified venom we know nothing about.

There are reptiles still alive today whose venom contains highly combustible chemical ingredients. Maybe Leviathan could light up those chemicals with another feature like the electric eel's 600 volts of electricity. The Bombardier has separate chambers for its chemicals, and when they mix it causes an explosion. If a known animal can make boiling hot smoke, why not fire? Stranger things have existed in the animal kingdom than breathing fire. There are many distinctive features we find in the fossil record that are now extinct. Eliminating the possibility of breathing fire just because we can't observe it today is closed-minded. As soon as we developed the right weaponry, I'm sure anything fire breathing would have been the first target for extermination. No wonder they aren't around for observation.

For those of you that just can't swallow the seemingly fairytale nature of this part of the description, let me mention that some scholars say this section is poetry and thus entirely figurative. Though I do not subscribe to the mythological interpretation of Leviathan, they have some valid points. For example: the words for nostril and anger coincide, so do the words for fire and destruction. These scholars say instead of imagining actual fire coming out of its nostrils, we should read that its anger explodes into destruction. My opinion is that a literal animal was used as an object lesson. Therefore, it has both literal and figurative meanings. If this section bothers you, do your own research into Canaanite mythology and see what you come up with. Whatever conclusion you come to, I hope you do not throw the whole Book of Job out with the fire-breathing Leviathan.

God begins this section by contrasting humans in relationship to Leviathan; we are puny weaklings in its sight.

"Can you reel in Leviathan with a hook or tie down his tongue with a rope?"

From the description of this creature the answer on both accounts is a resounding, no!  Rather than reeling it in, it would pull us under.  Like modern croc wrestlers, the first goal in restraining a fierce creature is tying up the snout so it can't bite.  That's just not going to happen with this guy.

"Can you put a rope in its nose or pierce its jaw with a hook?"

Again, putting a rope through its nose would be about controlling the animal and leading it where you want it to go. In many parts of the world, especially India and Asia, it is still common to use a rope through the nose as a primitive halter. Leviathan wasn't about to submit to such a thing.

There also doesn't seem to be any part of Leviathan that is easily pierced. The piercing of an animal's jaw with a hook would be about capture or containment.  It's not even plausible.

In contrast, Job feels both captive to God's whim and controlled by His sovereign will.  He feels he's without choice and without understanding of God's mysterious master-plan, like God has a rope through his nose or a hook in his jaw leading him around against his will.  Life is happening to him instead of him being an active participant.

"Will it lavish on you earnest prayers, or speak to you tenderly?  Will it make a covenant with you?  Will you take him to be our slave forever?"

Leviathan is free to do what he wants, when he wants.  He's slave to no one.   He doesn't ask permission or make deals.

Nothing is based on a relationship, not even an abusive, narcissistic one. He just steals, kills, and destroys according to his desire.

Note the tones of sarcasm. "Will he beg you sweetly?" Ridiculous.

"Will it amuse you like a caged songbird?"

And we wonder where the sarcastic, Jewish sense of humor comes from.

Some of you are correcting me right now for the redundant nature of the previous sentence. Others have their head cocked to the side with one eyebrow pointed to the ceiling wondering if I'm a racist. No, ask any Jewish comedian (like my husband); culturally, sarcasm is like breathing.

"Will you put it on a leash for your little girl?"

This absolutely *absurd* image is what finally struck through my thick skull! I finally allowed the possibility to dawn that the Book of Job was not what I had always assumed.

Imagine Job processing a fire-breathing dragon on a leash held by a little girl. His three daughters had just died in a horrific tragedy, but not so long ago they were little girls with chubby cheeks, unruly red hair, and bright eyes. The thought of one of his sweet, little innocents anywhere near a dragon would have caused an immediate and fierce emotional reaction in this overly protective father. Adding a leash wouldn't have changed anything. It is ludicrous to think Leviathan would be safe and docile under any conditions. Of course he wouldn't put it on a leash for his little girl!

God is using sarcasm to make a point. The use of sarcasm changes the whole perception of God's entire answer. Westerners are taught that sarcasm is rude and cruel. It's not politically correct. However, sarcasm is a staple of Semitic culture. It isn't just acceptable; a good grasp of sarcasm is the only way to function in society. Sarcasm isn't a modern invention. In fact, it's used frequently throughout the Bible (Exod 14:11, 1 Sam 21:15, 1 Kgs 18:27).

God used this type of drastic imagery in order to speak to Job in a way that he could understand the point. It was like defibrillation paddles to shock Job's thought pattern out of its rut of assumption. Unlike most use of sarcasm, its use was *for* Job, not against him. Job was such a cynic (God called him a "faultfinder, critic") that God was using his native language to communicate. God wasn't lecturing Job for being a schlep who didn't understand His motives. God wasn't just berating Job for questioning His methods. Nor was God simply making a statement about the way things are. Instead, He's using this sarcastic line of questioning to shatter Job's long held beliefs about control and use of force over unruly souls. God was pushing Job to the edges of his belief system and asking if his logic still worked.

Leviathan on a leash for a little girl to play with is preposterous. So is Job's belief that God controls violent offenders by jerking them around under his control. Humanity did not have the power to control Leviathan but, if He wanted to, God could control even this great beast. Yet God chooses not to. He wants willing volunteers. God does not rule His Kingdom through tyranny! That's a Leviathan trait, the direct opposite of God's way. God is the Supreme Being, but He does not use His sovereignty as a weapon of control.

Leviathan chooses to rebel and so do rebellious humans. They go their own way (Isa 53:6, Rom 10:3), yet God still has a plan for them. Their rebellion is not a surprise. It is not outside the limits God set for them. God's plan is for the knowledge of Him to fill the earth as the waters cover the sea (Gen 1:28, Isa 11:9). Knowledge of Him is the beginning of a real relationship. God intends for us all to reflect His loving kindness to the rest of creation, to bring everything into a deeper relationship. Leviathan does this in a negative way. It does not love, but God mercifully provides for it anyway. The rebellious show the world His merciful and compassionate nature through His grace toward them (Rom 9:22-23). God's sovereignty isn't simply about yanking His opposition around on a leash, but rather about revealing His supremacy by loving even rebellious creatures like Leviathan.

> "Will traders open it up and divide it among the merchants?"

Job felt like his friends cut him open and divided him up—and God did nothing to stop them. These friends were supposed to be leaders and teachers. They were priests of their people. They were supposed to comfort and encourage him. Instead, Job thought they were traders ready to serve him up at their first opportunity (Job 6:27). Would God treat him the same way? When you've been betrayed by the very people who should be protecting and encouraging you, it is easy to think so. Job, sitting in his pile of ashes scraping his worm infested skin, felt like it. Because he felt like it, did that make it so? Thankfully, he persevered until he understood the truth.

> "Can you fill its hide with harpoons or its head with fishing spears?"

No, God went on to answer the question for Job—and us—very clearly.

> "If you put your hand on it, you will remember the battle and never try to do it again! Oh, the false hope—don't even try to envision it! No one is fierce enough to waken it, yet what is it to set its face toward me?"

In Job 3:8, Job cursed the day he was born like a day was cursed when someone wakes Leviathan. Apparently, it's not something you'd want to attempt. Don't even try touching it. No one was brave enough to combat Leviathan head on and win. But did that make him greater than or even equal to God?

> "Who will confront me that I should restore everything under heaven to him? Indeed no! I fabricated it all by myself and spoke its power and grace, its value."

No, there isn't anything in creation able to wrest the kingdom from God. God will not relinquish His throne even to the mightiest rebel. God is the one who created and empowered everything. He is greater than all those who defy Him. He could have chosen not to make them or to destroy them. Instead He chose not to diminish the power, grace, or value of what He spoke into existence—even when He knew it would revolt.

> "Who can remove its facial array with its set of jaws? Who goes outdoors to face him; who swings wide the gate when those fearsome teeth are around? Its pride is in its rows of armor shut and sealed tightly together. They are so close to one another that no air can enter the space between them. They are so closely related that they stick, and catch and cannot be divided.

Its sneeze shines light, and its eyes are like the eyelids of the morning. Its mouth is a torch out of which escape flames of fire. His glowering breath will kindle and flames go out from his mouth. In its neck is strength. Those who meet it will jump in fear. Its pendulous flesh is as hard as cast iron which cannot be shaken. Its heart is like cast from stone, as hard as a piece of the depths. From its rising the mighty will fear him, even from the destruction of a near miss."

Overall, this section describes the superlative nature of this beast. This thing was the image of a fire-breathing hellion, powerful and destructive. When read literally, it had awesome armored plates, and probably creepy golden or red eyes like the color of sunrise, and spat fire at anyone who came near. If read figuratively the thing was still a monster. Proverbs 30:13 uses this idea of eyes with lifting eyelids as an idiom that means an angry, arrogant attitude that goes on to devour everything nearby. Leviathan embodies this Proverb. It was the epitome of arrogance at the dawn of its reign of terror. (Make an angry glare with your face; as your eyebrows press down feel your eyelids open wide to focus on your prey. It has that attitude all day every day.) This leads us to another idiom that we still use today. "Its pendulous flesh is as hard as cast iron." "Pendulous flesh" is a nice way of saying pudenda, i.e. "boy parts." The metal may have evolved over the years from iron, to brass, to steel, but the meaning is the same. Leviathan had huevos; he was scared of nothing. In contrast, there was no hero whose knees didn't tremble when faced with this beast. The world of men was left helpless at his power. Leviathan was the ultimate tyrant.

"It cannot be over taken with a sword, nor will a spear hold up when thrown at its armor. It considers iron like straw and bronze like rotten wood. It doesn't run away when barraged with arrows; they are but straw. Sling stones are like leaves. Clubs it considers stubble and laughs at a shaken javelin."

This section describes Leviathan's defensive strategy. With all that armor, he didn't really need one. Imagine crocodilian armor scaled up on something roughly the size of a school bus. Leviathan is invincible to any primitive weapon you could launch at it. No amount of lethal force is going to take it down.

Job described, in chapter 6, that he felt like the arrows of the Almighty were in him. He then asked "Do I have the strength of stone? Is my flesh bronze?" (NIV). He also asked, "Am I a sea monster or a dragon that you must place me under guard?" (Job 7:12, NLT). It's as if he were asking, "Am I as strong or as impenetrable as a Leviathan that you attack me like this? Do you think I can survive it? What have I ever done that makes you want to destroy me like a fearsome, evil beast?" God is taking Job's own example to the utmost extreme to make a point. Job is just about to have an epiphany as to what that point is. There is just a little more description first.

"Under it are claws as sharp as potshards which spread scratches in the mud. It makes the depths boil like ointment put in a cauldron. Behind it is a shining path; one would think the deep had gray hair."

To me, this section sounds like the hunting strategy of the Spinosaurus. It spent its time fishing the waters often by waiting on river banks to snatch prey from the water like a bear using its front claws and jaws. Its intimidating, 6-10 inch front claws would have left sharp impressions in the mud. Some translations say its underbelly makes sharp impressions in the mud like a threshing sledge. This would also fit how the Spinosaurus used its hind legs to propel its body over the mud like a penguin over snow or a mud-surfing croc. Suffice it to say, Leviathan left scary prints in the mud that would make going for water a terrifying experience.

Maybe what is being described as making the sea boil is caused by kicking up the river bed to dislodge fish hiding in the sand, or bubble netting fish in the water like a whale, or maybe it had a method of deploying its pyrotechnics underwater. Its fishing technique or maybe just its sail sticking up out of the water left a signature, tell-tale wake in the water as it swam. Everybody knew to run away as fast as they could.

Now, the moment we've all been waiting for: Job has his eureka moment!

God finishes his description, "No dominion on Earth can make it do anything. It is completely without fear. It looks haughtily as king over all the sons of pride."

Job replied, "I know that you can do all things; no purpose of yours can be thwarted" (NIV).

The meaning is lost if you stop for the night at the end of chapter 41 and start the next day on chapter 42. One moment follows directly after the other. Job is answering God, "Yes, I know that he is disobedient, terrifying, and prideful. Yet now I see and understand that though You have the power to crush Leviathan or force it to do anything You want, You do not cut it off from your plan or have a wicked plot against it. Even Leviathan cannot cut short Your purpose with its rebellion."

The first few times I read the Book of Job, many of the pivotal moments in the story were lost on me. I read them through according to my religious preconceptions—blah, blah, blah—waiting for a spectacular revelation of some big secret. Duh, of course God's plan can't be thwarted; God is great. Job's been saying that through the whole story. This moment seemed like no big deal. I didn't understand the dramatic shift in the rest of the book. It wasn't until I put myself in Job's shoes and tried to read it from his perspective that something new struck me. God has spent a whole chapter explaining Leviathan's terrible rebellion and inability to be controlled, yet God's plan can't be thwarted. Since Leviathan rebels against the good nature of the world God created, either God planned for Leviathan to be evil, or obedient slaves are not the ultimate plan. God is not the author of evil (1 Cor 14:33, Jas 1:13). Therefore, the second statement must true. A Santa Claus god whose sole purpose is to control our behavior with reward and punishment is a woefully shallow misunderstanding of the nature of God and His purpose.

In the example of Leviathan, Job finally realized God's message. God said the same thing ten different ways with ten different animals. James 5:11 tells us the point of everything God said, "…the unfolding conclusion of the Lord, you have perceived; that extremely full of intense, visceral affection is the Lord, and compassionate." God is revealing His "eternal power and divine nature" to the world through every part of creation—even the rebellious Leviathan (Rom 1:20, 1 Cor 13, 1 John 4). He will fill the whole earth with His likeness and image. This is His original Genesis 1 plan that cannot be thwarted. The image we are all supposed to portray is one of kindness and humility, not tyranny and vengeance (Col 3:1-17).

There are several lessons we can take away from Leviathan. First, God has the power to destroy and to create, yet this power is wielded by love, not hate. In fact, the Bible tells us that it takes a great force of evil built up for a long period of time to overcome God's pity and compassion (Ps 78:38-39, Hos 10-11, Jer 13). Even then, after their consequences are met, God relents and has compassion once again (Hos 14, Jer 12:15). God is not out to control us like slaves or manipulate us like children. Instead, the motive of God is to know and be known. Everything He is doing is to bring us back into the relationship He intended for us before the creation of the world: free, mature, voluntary, and powerful.

Secondly, even Leviathan, as rebellious as it is, is cared for and unduly blessed by God. The Almighty does not have evil intentions even toward those who have missed the bull's eye. He's not out to break the teeth of His enemies. God did not pre-write a story with bad guys simply to show off how big and strong He is by crushing them. Evil will be dealt with in the end, but humanity is not God's intended target of judgment. Hell was made for Satan and the rebellious ones who followed him (Matt 25:41); hence the repeated warnings to repent and leave the kingdom of this world.

Leviathan will eventually be held accountable for every drop of blood shed by his violence (Gen 9). However, at this moment in the story of Job, Leviathan had an opportunity to make choices. Even today the rebellious have a new day to make choices. We cannot control their choices. Still, they won't get away with rebellion forever; this is just the middle of their story. Even if they die happy in their beds, what comes next will be a rude awakening. Their punishment is not our responsibility (Rom 12:19-20, Heb 10:30).

Our responsibility now is to make good choices.  In fact, it is in taking responsibility that our true power lies.  As long as we try to pawn off responsibility on someone else, we are giving our power away.  If we don't take responsibility for our choices, we are powerless.  Whoever is responsible for us has our power.  That's why tyrants like Satan are always offering to take care of us.  They say it's free and for our safety, when really it's for our captivity.  God endowed us with the power to make responsible choices.  We need to stand up and use our will for the good of all!

As we react to the trauma of life, we have the opportunity to realize God wrote us as heroes in His story.  That's not just for Bible characters, martyrs, or missionaries.  We can stand up and fill the role or simply let the opportunity pass us by.  The choice is there for us to make.

God can use even the violence of a Leviathan to our advantage.  Satan's very attacks against us can be what strengthens our ability to conquer him.  When the dust clears and the wounds heal, we will know that we can overcome anything (1 Sam 17:32-37, Phil 4:13).  We truly are princes and princesses of God.

God is still God even in the chaos.  Even if our worst fear comes true, it is only the middle of the story.  God makes beauty from ashes.  He doesn't make ashes, but is willing to take the risk of offering choice knowing that He will have to clean them up.  Why?  Because relationship without choice is not love, it's slavery.  Since God is love; He wants a relationship with even the worst of the worst, and He won't let a little chaos get in the way of love.

The moment Job realized God wants to show the world His affectionate and compassionate nature, he was set free from his slavery to the Law. There was an immediate change in his course of action. He was no longer afraid of being punished. He knew God loved him—not just as the ambiguous Shaddi in the sky concept, but him personally. God's love isn't just for the lineage of the "chosen" heir; it is for *all* creation including Edomites like Job. No matter what came next, God was for him not against him.

Chapter 14

Sugar, and Spice, and Everything Nice!

"The Lord blessed the latter part of Job's life more than the former part. ...And so Job died, an old man and full of years." (Job 42:12-17, NIV)

At the beginning of the book we see Job obsessively following the rules for fear of being punished and in order to earn blessings. God called him a "faultfinder." Job held himself to a strict standard and was highly critical of everyone and everything he didn't think lived up to that standard. At the end of the book we see him go far beyond what the rules require. We see him love and forgive because he has been loved and forgiven by God. We see him become gracious because God's love, joy, and peace are flowing out of him. The very thing Job had been trying so hard to gain and maintain through works was fulfilled in him through relationship. Authority, value, joy, and confidence are now Job's. He is without fear or compulsion. He is safe in the eyes of God.

Job's new life began with personal restoration. He had lived distant from God. As an Edomite descended from rejected Esau instead of beloved Jacob, he felt he wasn't included in the promise of Messiah. God did not love him and certainly not his half-Hittite family. Yet nothing was further from the truth. If God loved the wild donkey, the wild ox, and even Leviathan, then God surely loved Job. He definitely had his own role to play in the Promise story—it just wasn't as Messiah's ancestor.

Job's restoration started with repentance. After realizing God's love, Job immediately repented for slandering the character of God. He said:

> You asked, "Who is this that obscures my plans without knowledge?" Surely I spoke of things I did not understand, things too wonderful for me to know. You said, "Listen now, and I will speak; I will question you, and you shall answer me."
>
> My ears had heard of you but now my eyes have seen you. Therefore, I despise myself and repent in dust and ashes" (Job 42:3-6, NIV).

Job states his offense was that he obscured the plans of God. God's plan was for each of us to fill the earth with His true likeness (Gen 1:26). Job fell short of being the glory of God by presenting a warped image of Him. Job missed the bull's eye set for all humanity. He sinned.

I have heard Job's and the Chief's theology quoted and used to prove certain ideas about God. That should never happen. Everything Job or his friends said previous to this moment must be examined carefully to find the lies mixed into the truth. The Father of Lies was their source of "truth" from the onset of the story (Job 4:12-21). Satan rarely deceives with pure fiction; he mixes together good and evil until they are indistinguishable. The Deceiver used their religion to push them away from God. Job and his friends were sincere when they proclaimed the harsh and conceited nature of God, but that does not make what they said true. Job said that he was grieved for his old way of thinking about God. He repented of it! Therefore, his old way of thinking should not enter our own theology.

If we use other scriptures to add a little color to his statement, Job's repentance could read something like this:

> I'm so sorry, God, for obscuring your purpose to testify to all the world of your extreme, visceral affection and compassion for your creation. That is a concept far beyond what I could have ever imagined. You responded to my plea for an audience just like I asked. You came and showed me personally your character—your mercy and compassion. I thought I knew everything about you, but I was only going off of what I had heard. Now I have seen you for myself, and I am so grieved over my misconception of you and your intention for creation. I must express my gut wrenching sorrow for telling others untruths about who you are. (Jas 5:11, Job 13:20-22, 42:3-6)

Whenever we have an encounter with God we can do one of two things: reject Him (which requires nothing on our part), or accept Him. Accepting Him requires us to change our way of thinking and feeling, which in turn changes our way of acting. By saying he rejected himself (or some versions say despised himself), Job was not devaluing himself. He was rejecting his soul's old, despised belief system and accepting the new, beautiful truth he now understood. In the past, Job believed God was a faultfinder, and his actions followed suit. He used the rules to criticize others instead of for personal growth in love and respect. But now, his spiritual understanding was opened to what his mind and heart could not perceive on their own. God is not a faultfinder (1 Cor

13:5). He loves even those who have faults. Job thought his self-righteousness imitated the image of God, but in reality it fell short of love. Knowing the truth made his heart ache over his old self. This is the perfect picture of true repentance—a whole soul makeover. His change of belief made him a new creation (2 Cor 5:17, Gal 6:15).

God didn't rant or sentence Job to penance. Instead, He immediately went on to address Job as "My servant Job" (Job 42:7-9). This term is not demeaning at all. First, in God's kingdom servant is the highest position one can attain (Phil 2). Second, it is a term used to label the people of God. It denotes a very intimate relationship to Him as evidenced by God listening to his prayers. By calling him servant, God put Job on the same level as one of the "chosen people" like Abraham, Moses, David, and the nation of Israel (Gen 26:24, Num 12:7, 2 Sam 3:18, Isa 41:8, 44:1, 21). He was saying now you are like Me; you're my child—a servant leader. It's as if God put His arm around Job and introduced him to everyone as His very own. The funny thing is, God viewed Job like this from the beginning; Job just wasn't aware of it (Job 1:8, 2:3).

After personal restoration, Job enjoyed social restoration. He became the intercessor that God always intended for leadership to be. Job responded to God's quick forgiveness by forgiving his friends. He didn't berate his friends, instead he prayed for them to be forgiven. Everyone who abandoned him in his time of trouble returned bringing comfort and gifts.

Next, Job experienced financial restoration. "God blessed the latter part of his life more than the former." Job got twice as much stuff as he had to start off with. The next couple of verses illustrate that Job no longer used stuff to measure his blessings. Financial wealth is not the reason James declared God merciful and compassionate.

Job's response to financial restoration was not to puff up his chest and gloat about how God loved him again; nor was it to hoard everything for himself. In a time when women were just as often classified as possessions as they were people, Job gave an inheritance to his daughters. Without regard to public opinion or established protocol, Job responded to God's generosity with generosity. He used his stuff as a tool to lift up those whom others saw as weak and lowly (Luke 16:9).

Job also had marital restoration. It had been almost two decades since he and his wife were intimate enough to produce children, something drastically changed. Since Job had seven more sons and three more daughters after his first ten children had all grown into adulthood, one of two conclusions can be made about his marriage; either something miraculous happened with his first wife, or he was blessed with a new one.

He and his wife had a lot of healing to do. She told him to "curse God and die." He retorted by calling her a "stupid, morally depraved woman"—not the most loving and kind of marriage relationships.

Obsessive rule-followers can tend toward a critical, rigid way of treating others—especially when someone under their authority acts morally depraved or stupid. The fact that he spoke the truth harshly to her gives us a glimpse of this. It may have been true, but it also made her feel like garbage.

Job's angry words toward his wife while legally justified were not in the likeness of God. This outburst under pressure reveals the character of a legalistic, faultfinder's heart. Job held himself to a high standard and would tolerate no less in the people who surrounded him. This legalism creates a divide between people. The self-righteous one exalts himself, and the one scorned feels belittled. The gulf in self-worth is insurmountable. It is death to any team, especially a marriage.

Yet here at the end of Job, he and his wife have ten more children. It is amazing his wife was physically able to have ten kids after her first ten had already grown to maturity. (It's possible. After all, twins run in the family—so does childbearing at a late age.) The miracle however, was the deep healing that would have had to take place between these two. Most marriages which lose children go on to fail, not improve—especially if Job's wife blamed him for their loss. Even before the tragedy, they hadn't produced children for at least as long as it took the youngest to grow up. If his wife suddenly started to have children again, something had changed in their personal habits that produced those children.

What was that change? Indulge me a little speculation from a woman's point of view. Job was a new man with a different heart. The result of a changed heart is changed actions toward the people around us. If he began treating his wife like the treasure she was rather than a legal contract trapping him to a "foolish woman," she would respond in kind.

For instance, his faithfulness to her would be a matter of love rather than an obligation to a "covenant with [his] eyes not to look at a woman" (Job 32:1). The change would occur not only because of love for his wife, but also out of respect for all women. Faithfulness would prevail because women would mean something totally different to him. He could love and defend all women like he would his own mother or sister or daughter. A pretty girl would no longer be a means of self-satisfaction. She would be another soul who needs the love of God. His pity for a woman's broken sense of value would dull any personal desire to gratify himself—even if she actively used her body as a tool to gain power or attention. He would no longer be simply strong arming his pleasure center; God's love for her would squelch a desire to use her. Lustful thoughts could quickly be captured by the love and compassion of God rather than spinning into obsession which leads to a selfish act.

His compassion and respect toward his realm would draw his wife's admiration. His faithfulness and love toward her would awaken her feelings for him. When a woman feels like a beautiful treasure to an admirable man, it creates a need to express those feelings to the one who made her feel this way. Well... whew! Let's just say that Job created an environment in which his wife was able to thrive—even at her age. There was a lot of healing that needed to happen between these two. It may not have happened instantly, but it all started because Job was loved by God, and in turn he loved his wife.

We do not have to wait for tragedy to strike before taking the first step toward restoration. Someone has to go first and break the cycle of hurt, even if the other person doesn't deserve it. The one who knows they are loved by God is accountable to take responsibility for the relationship. Reach out to those with whom we are in a broken relationship, whether spouse, parent, sibling or otherwise. Love and honor first, require nothing in return—even if they have an obligation to do so.

Since there's no mention of a new wife, I like to believe Job's marriage was restored. While not specifically pointed out, Job's new children are evidence of a renewed (or at least new) marital relationship along with all of the other blessings listed.

The fruit of their reunion was plentiful, seven sons and three daughters. Children were listed separately from all Job's other blessings. I think that's because they were a result of

Job's heart change, not God handing him something like everything else on the list.

It does not surprise me that the number of his sons was equal to God's number of completion. Interestingly, for some reason his sons are left unnamed. This makes the detailed description of his daughters all the more fascinating.

In ancient cultures it was the sons who were important. Everyone felt blessed by sons; girls were a responsibility, another mouth to feed. At best, they were a commodity to be traded for wealth or status, an opportunity for treaty and alliance. Yet here, the girls are named and the boys are not.

The names of his girls tell us a little about how Job was feeling when they were born. In this era people did not just choose a baby name for its melodic value but for its meaning.

First is Jemimah, in Hebrew "*Yemimah*." We are not totally sure what this name means. Some say it means, "Dove." Because "*yowm*" means warmth of the day, it's an idea that associates her with warmth, affection and sweetness, hence a dove. It could also mean "strong springs." This is the meaning I lean toward because of the significance of it to Job's family. Anah, Esau's father-in-law, found "*yemim*" in the wilderness, and it sustained their herds (Gen 36:24). The first part of "*yemim*" is "*yam*" or "*yom*." It's something flowing like time or water, hence a day, spring, or river. This is paired with "mem" meaning water. Together we get "flowing water." A strongly flowing source of water would have been an extremely precious resource to this man with so much livestock. A spring isn't dependent on the fickle weather and cannot be dammed or diverted by an enemy—and they wouldn't have to face Leviathan to get a drink! His springs were a huge part of Job's success because they were always faithfully, constantly flowing. Jemimah was refreshment, healing, and sustenance in a dry and weary world—a source of true wealth and power.

Whether her name meant "Dove" or "Spring," both express his affectionate, new relationship with the love of God in the form of his sweet, baby girl. His little Jemimah embodied provision from the Living Water Himself. She was priceless treasure to him.

His next daughter was Keziah. Her name is a premium member of the cinnamon family. It would have been an exotic, valuable import. Besides making food pleasurable, its oil was used for fragrance and medicinal purposes. It is a good anti-microbial (germ fighter) and helps the body deal with sugar. Job named his daughter after an expensive, exotic spice that added pleasure, health, and protection to the world.

His last daughter is Keren-Happuch. Keren means, "Horn or Container." Horns were associated symbolically with authority and power. Happuch is a shiny, dark stone called Antimony. It was used in cosmetics applied to the eyes of queens and nobles. It was thought that this dark, kohl make-up could protect eyes from the sun, heal eye problems, and shield from "the evil eye." Keren-Happuch was a "Valuable Container of Beauty." She didn't just have the beauty of a dumb, shiny rock; she had the beauty of a noble woman who possessed the power to strengthen, heal, and protect. In a world where women—especially the youngest in the family— were not always highly esteemed, this name showed just what a jewel she was to her father. Job honored the youngest and least worthy in the family with a name of great power and respect.

Each of his daughters was given a name that said they were loved and cherished by their father. They had inherent value and power of their own. Their names reveal the affectionate heart of their father toward them and toward God. They were his Sugar, Spice, and Everything-Nice. Job's regard for women drastically changed because his heart had changed. He was no longer a fault-finder, but a man who encourages and empowers.

I love the note that says, "Nowhere in all the land were there found women as beautiful as Job's daughters" (Job 42:15, NIV). The wording leaves it open so that both the literal and figurative interpretation of beautiful could be inferred. The honor from their father radiated inside until it shone on the outside. The glow of inner confidence is one of the most comely attributes on any woman's face. These girls knew their true value, and it showed. An internal sense of value dampers the need to be petulant, needy, or manipulative. They were beautiful inside and out.

Job went beyond just saying his daughters were highly valuable. He proved it publicly by giving them an inheritance with their brothers! Job had seven sons. Usually the eldest son inherited the bulk of the father's fortune and his position of authority. The other boys got something, but the girls would have to get married. Their husbands would ensure and control their fortunes. Job gave his girls "like inheritance" to their brothers. He legally told the world his girls were just as valuable and responsible as his boys. He didn't overcompensate either (the way feminism often does). He didn't elevate his girls and put down his boys. Each of his children were treated as equals. This was a huge departure in a family where Abraham gave his sons gifts and sent them off to live in the East while Isaac inherited the bulk of everything. His girls became independently wealthy, free from the need to marry into a position of power.

Job showed he loved his children all the same—even those for whom he didn't legally have an obligation to do anything.

Job was no longer just following the rules; he was being love. His actions were a manifestation of the way God treats humans. Job's extreme, visceral affection for his daughters was a direct reflection of God's compassion for creation—all creation. Job's actions foreshadow the way Jesus treated women when He arrived on the scene. He lifted them up to a place of honor and value, and then empowered them with freedom. I'm no feminist, but that gets me excited.

Like Job, we can look for ways to lift up others. We can value those that society says are not worth the effort and empower those who have never felt like they were able. It should start in our homes and spill over into the world around us. When God is our God, we have no excuse to withhold value from another human being. We don't have to agree on everything to assess value to someone else. It is only Satan who makes the claim that people different from us are sub-human. It doesn't matter if they have a different skin tone, a different gender, a different religion, denomination, or whatever; we are all God's creation. Since value is set by what someone will pay for a thing, we should recognize that God already set their value exactly the same as ours. He was willing to give His Son in exchange for us all. Our concept of rank is just vestigial wilderness rhetoric. The greatest in the Kingdom of God is a servant. He serves with wisdom, not simply doing what his subjects want, but what is best for them—even if it makes them cry out in temporary pain.

What is the result of Job's life altering heart change? Job lived an astounding 140 years after his trouble. He got to watch his sons, and his Sugar, Spice, and Everything-Nice grow up and have children of their own. He had the chance to hold his grandchildren and great-children. He was able to care for and teach those under his authority for more years than most people. "Job died an old man full of days" (Job 42:17). This can mean both that he lived all the days God planned for him to live, and that he lived abundantly all his days.  His life was fully satisfied and satisfying.  Job died a rich man, but I'm sure if you asked him he would tell you it wasn't the number of sheep in his pasture that made all of his days satisfying.  It was the fullness of his relationships that the Book of Job notes with the fullness of his days.

# Chapter 15

## Lessons from Job

"Peace I leave with you; my peace I give you. I do not give to you as the world gives. Do not let your hearts be troubled and do not be afraid." (John 14:27, NIV)

If we take all of these lessons from lion to Leviathan, and put them into context against the whole Bible, we can see God's loving character from the Old Testament to the New. We need to realign ourselves and our belief systems to it.

When I first read the Book of Job, I was looking for answers: Why was my life was so hard and unsatisfying? Why was all this happening to me? I expected the Book of Job to clearly explain why bad things happen to "good" people. I wanted answers neatly numerated and alliterated like a predigested Sunday sermon. I was disappointed because Job isn't like that. It's messy and raw.

The problem was my questions were me-centric, focused on explanations for my immediate problems. I needed to zoom out and ask God-centric questions about the big picture:

Who did all those horrible things to Job? It was not God; it was Satan.

What did God let Satan do? God let Satan destroy every worldly thing from which Job derived honor and security. Satan repossessed everything Job spent his life acquiring by means of religious currency.

Why did God allow Satan to destroy Job's world? Satan's motive was to obliterate Job and shake the faith of everyone who heard the story. God's motive for allowing Satan to exercise his limited legal authority was to set Job free from the fear caused by legalistic religion. God wanted Job to experience abundant life (John 10:10). He desired a real relationship.

How did Satan gain authority over Job? It was a legal transaction. First, Satan prowled around looking for Job's fears. His research yielded that Job was doing good works in exchange for blessing and protection. Job deeply feared humiliation among his social and religious peers. Next, the Accuser filed suit in the Court of Heaven. God indeed saw that Job was not doing good works simply to express the generosity of God's love. This was the evidence Satan used to prove Job did not serve the Lord God, but rather the god of this world—himself.

Satan legally won possession of Job's life account. Satan held the debt for every moment Job spent in religious activity done to gain honor and safety instead of from a loving relationship with God. He immediately went out and demanded the price be paid for Job's purchases of self-esteem and empowerment from the company store.

The fact that Job had only ever shopped in the religious section did not negate his debt to the Deceiver who sells religion in place of relationship. Under the law of religion, you get what you pay for. You reap what you sow. You give because what goes around comes around. If you sow a good work in fear, you will reap a harvest corrupted by fear.

Religion is meant to guide the immature into a relationship with God; it was never meant to be a system of living apart from Him.

In contrast, the Kingdom of God is based solely on a state of being. It is because I AM. We do because I AM (Exod 3:14, 1 John 4:19). Generosity is a matter of character, not currency, not for something in return.

Job thought religious activity had bought him blessing and protection. Instead, religion gave Satan the legal grounds to repossess everything Job had worked for.

When Job's world turned upside down, he said God gives and takes away (Job 1:21). He got one thing wrong: god. It was not the LORD who took anything; it was the god of this world at work. The Lord gave good gifts. Satan proved that Job viewed those gifts as payment for good works. Satan is the wage payer, the slave driver. If we are looking for something in return for our good works, we are still under the law of sin and death. Satan was his god. While Job thought he served the Lord God; he was actually serving the god of this world according to the Law.

The book of Job doesn't offer answers for why God makes life so hard because it is not God who is out to hurt us. In fact, why tragedy strikes is often too murky to sort out no matter where we look for the source. God, Satan, and man all have a role to play in what is happening now. Blaming one without taking into consideration of the other forces leaves our answers lopsided and insufficient. God has delegated limited authority to others. Pain most often occurs when He lifts his hand of protection and allows the lesser powers in this world to assert their own will to a greater degree.

The whole point of the Book of Job is not to explain why bad things happen, but to show that God loves us. He has extreme, visceral affection and compassion for all, good and bad alike. He is working to develop a relationship with us. Our value is not based on merit according to the Law, but is found in the character of God and who He declares us to be. He has given each of us a role to play in spreading the image of God throughout creation. Some will fulfill His will in a positive way; they will reflect God's image of love by loving those under their care (like the wild goat, the stork, and Behemoth). Others reject His perfect will and instead display His image like a photographic negative; they are not loving, but rather through them God demonstrates His mercy and compassion for the unlovable (like the wild donkey, the wild ox, the ostrich, and Leviathan).

If we look carefully, the whole world displays His love for all of us. When we are finally able to see the character of God, everything else makes sense. Trust overwhelms fear (1 John 4:18).

Yet we still live in a broken world. Until the wilderness is destroyed and the Kingdom of God is all that exists, we will experience pain. It's heart wrenching and tragic. However, laying blame doesn't help us deal with heartache even if we could figure out who's at fault.

What matters more than blame is what we do with the mess. We can choose to trust God and "rejoice always" or, we can try to force the world to comply with our comfort zone. The latter is unsustainable for very long. It just doesn't work. If we want the ability to rejoice without faking it, we'll need a new perspective on our circumstances. Everything that happens to us can become an empowering experience. It can make us wiser, stronger, more flexible, empathetic, and compassionate leaders in the Kingdom of God.

The farther I get down this road of trust, the deeper the rabbit hole gets. Belief started with trusting Jesus died for my sins, but it has grown into a hardcore assurance that sacrificial love really is the only way to find true happiness. The Kingdom of God isn't just a churchy quip we flippantly rattle off in a stuffy, old prayer. It is the original plan, and it is powerfully coming to fruition whether we're ready or not. Love wins, and only those who voluntarily participate get to abide in it forever. I want to be a part of it! Thank God He sent Christ to make that possible!

It's not that I think I'm anything extraordinary, so God should pick me. In fact, I believe my ordinariness is one of the greatest assets to my mission (1 Cor 1:27). Yet God believed in me enough to spend His life on me. All I can do in response is believe Him, trust that He has equipped me, get out there, and follow His lead.

God believes in you equally as much. I believe in you too! No matter where you are starting, if you are yoked with God, you can do whatever He has called you to do. I believe the whole church can wake from her slumber. I believe we win! I am not even an optimist. The reality of God simply supersedes the empirical world! The spiritual world is the real reality. The physical world just acts it out like players on a stage. If we can get our souls on track with God's reality, then our satisfaction will follow suit.

The ability to trust God would make something amazing out of my ugliest pain changed my whole view of life. The idea of having a dynamic relationship with the One who can sculpt me into something beautiful inundated all of my problems. Yes, I still pray, "Lead me not into trials, but deliver me from the Evil One" (Matt 6:13). I'd rather learn from study and have as little struggle as possible. But if trouble comes, I know I will be a better version of me on the other side of it. Now the abundant life doesn't ebb and flow with the ease of the journey. God and I are walking through this life together. He isn't far off in the heavens; He is comforting and guiding here and now.

The definition of danger changes as we relinquish control. Safety no longer means that nothing bad will ever happen in this fallen world. On the contrary, we are told that "in this world we will have trouble" (John 16:33). This change in thinking allows us to stop trying to make others choose to protect us. They often can't or won't. Instead, safety means freedom from Satan's traps; we can have peace of mind because we trust God to work out benefit regardless of circumstances. Trouble is opportunity for us to learn to be sovereign over our own thoughts, feelings, and actions toward others, to become more like Christ. This in turn empowers us to be greater public servants in the Kingdom of God.

Jesus said that "God cares when the sparrows fall to the ground... So don't be afraid; you are worth more than many sparrows" (Matt 10:28-31). He did not say that he would never let a sparrow fall; rather, He would care for them when it happened. If the sparrows never leave the nest, they will never learn to fly. God wants us to learn to fly freely; it's in our DNA.

As the world is now, the next step in maturity is often a painful or bothersome process like falling from the nest. Learning to crawl takes time and practice, and probably at least one scuffed knee. Learning to walk takes falling down many times. Learning to eat with a utensil gets messy (some of us still shouldn't wear white). Learning to ride a bike will surely involve a scrape or two. Getting new teeth means losing the old ones. Learning to be a good friend will undoubtedly involve some emotional scars. Thanks to Eve, growing up is a bloody process (Gen 3:16). Maturity takes time, practice, intention, and a willingness to get back up; yet no one would say it isn't worth it.  We know something is very wrong when it doesn't occur.

Maturing spiritually takes no less effort, falling down, and getting back up.  But we are not left to stumble through it on our own.  God will teach us how to rule our world well.  Yoked with Him, we can know how to take hold of the wilderness and make it more like the Garden.  He will show us when to act and when to wait, when to speak and when to be quiet, when to sow, when to let grow, and when to reap.  Avoiding the pain of growing up will only lead to a different kind of pain and ineptitude.

The peace we are all looking for is not found in perfect, circumstantial safety and security but in the deep confidence that "The Lord is near" (Ps 34:18, 145:18).  He is listening to our prayers and working on our behalf to make us His heirs to this world.  We can have peace which surpasses understanding (Phil 4:4-9).  It comes from a relationship with God.

Philippians 4:5-6 explains further how this sense of security works.  In a crisis we can't try to control the people around us.  Instead, we should talk to God like a friend about what we are going through.  Ask Him why.  Tell Him how we feel and talk about what a good solution would be.  Is there a part we should play?  Then trust Him with a thankful heart to do what is best, whether action or inaction, rescue or endurance.  Trust Him even when those He assigned to take action on His behalf fail us.  He will deal with that too.

Philippians 4:8-9 tells us how to accomplish this peace.  Rather than focusing on the problem and how the people around us are making it worse, focus on the truth.  Do not only see with physical, mental, and emotional senses; see with spiritual senses too.  It's impossible to just stop thinking about the problems of life.  We must replace those thoughts with something new to obsess about.  What is true?  What is noble? What is right? What is pure, lovely, admirable, excellent, or praise worthy? To find these in the darkness of our situation, we cannot look around us; we must look up. By continuously marinating the truth in our mind, our belief system begins to change. In turn, our feelings begin to change followed by our actions.

What is the truth about God? We can know exactly what God is like when we look at Jesus. God is Love (1 John 4). He passionately loves you. He wants what is best for us and is continually working to accomplish it. He will go to any length necessary to win us back from the Enemy—including die for us.

Even if we've made bad choices that hurt, God still loves us and can heal the pain. We can overcome the darkest of problems because we're not in it alone. God's strength is there for us. He's willing to give us eyes to see a new path and the strength to choose to stay on it.

God can heal us from pain inflicted by other people's terrible choices just as thoroughly as He can soothe our own failures and self-doubt. God can transform our hurt and give us new life. The hurt we suffer as a result of living in a fallen world is not greater than the power of God to heal. The pain is very real and doesn't go away just because we ignore it or wallow in it. Bring it to Him. Ask Him how it's possible to make anything good from this heartbreak you've gone through. Like a sculptor with clay, He will remake this mess into a work of art named you. Only God's love can take the dark ashes of our soul and make them into something beautiful (Isa 61). He can repurpose what Satan intended to destroy you and use it to teach you to fly. Knead His love into all of the dry cracks the fires of life have caused. After your heart is healed, He can bring people into your life to see your beauty and inspire them to go through the same healing process (2 Cor 1).

Complete healing comes from a personal relationship with Love. Short of being visited by God in a whirlwind, the best way to get to know the real God is to read His Word and talk to Him. Get to know Him for yourself. Seek a true relationship with God. Don't read the Bible looking for a formula to get what you want or for a spiritual high. Only then will you be able to trust Him and breathe.

Love, joy, and peace flow freely in a relationship with God. It starts with rejecting our old self and receiving a new belief system. Our new relationship with God is evidenced by a change of heart from loving-self to loving-outside-of-self.

Love is powerful, yet confusing. It's utterly impossible unless we daily seek God in the matter. Love isn't just sappy niceness; there are many other facets to explore. Love is anything but black and white and can't be put in a box. Only with God does the vivid palette of love truly come to life. Sometimes love offers free gifts to gain trust; other times love draws boundaries and says no. It offers choice and discipline to grow and mature the subject of affection. Neither approach lacks love. Love is always working in the best interest of others, not self.

Merely following the Law does not bring life abundantly. Like Job, those who are religious rule-followers mix doing the right thing with the wrong reason. They follow the Law with the purpose of attaining what they want in the kingdom of self. This will lead to completely missing out on life abundantly. Job was freed from this paradox by an encounter with the True God. He allowed the love God had for the unlovable to quicken his heart to life.

The Book of Job isn't a glitzy story about how God rescues us through miracles. I am an eye witness that it can and does still happen, but that facet of love is written in other books, for other audiences. Pigeonholing God into a box that requires Him to acquiesce to our comfort zone is a dangerous faith to hold. Eventually, God will act outside the formula we've set up for Him, and that can be life shattering.

Instead, the Book of Job deals with working through the reality of a situation when that miraculous rescue does not happen. Hold your head up; He has not abandoned you! The birth of new life, the strength of endurance, the confidence of victory, the glow of compassion, and the blaze of passion are often only achieved through adversity. These are no less miraculous in our weary, fearful lives than a dramatic rescue would have been. God can use the very heartbreak we experience in this broken world to make us into the kings and queens He always planned for us to be.

My life has not been all cherries and roses. I have experienced tragedies. Some of them were the direct result of my own choices. Some of them were the direct result of other people's choices. Most of them were the indirect result of Adam and Eve's choice that produced a fallen world. I do not believe any of them resulted from God sitting in heaven, gleefully tossing lightning bolts in my direction because I sinned; He didn't store up a bucket of hail just waiting for the right moment to tip it over. He did, however, solemnly authorize the consequences for poor choices made. Nothing has been random or hidden from Him. He could see the conception of the matter before there was even a flutter of awareness on my part. The consequences He sovereignly chose were all lovingly aimed at setting me free from my love of self. I no longer need to trade my soul to the masters for tidbits.

The same goes for the rest of humanity. Satan aims to destroy us with the consequences of our actions. But God will weave good things out of the mess if we trust Him to make us more like Love (Rom 8:28).

The knowledge that choice will affect my world does not leave me terrified of a world spinning into chaos. I know my God sovereignly holds the balance of justice. There are governors on choice; those controls are called consequences. Only He knows how far to allow us to diverge from the bull's eye. He is the One who set up those boundaries and knows their purpose. Only He has the wisdom to decide when it is best to act to change the outcome, and when it is best not to act and allow the consequences for choice to play out.

Could He have written history differently? Sure, but I am convinced that He has done, and will always do, what is best for both victims and offenders. It is hypocritical to condemn God for not eliminating evil on our time table while complaining He is too judgmental and harsh when our own consequences come. I've heard Him criticized in the same breath for not doing away with evil and for preaching about the Judgment Day to come when pain is utterly destroyed. We complain that He is too controlling in our lives and that He isn't controlling enough when it comes to other people's bad behavior. We have to remember God is for us, not against us. He's for us *all*!

At this point in time, history is still unfolding. God has a plan, and it will not be thwarted. The plan was set out in Genesis chapter one. Humanity is to rule the earth in the image and likeness of God so that all of creation will know and love Him. We are the glory of God. The word "glory" means "to express the proper opinion of someone." Like a sculpture, a photo, or a mirror, our lives portray what we believe about God. We can depict Him as He is or be an example of His mercy and compassion.  Either way, the knowledge of God is coming to fruition like an avalanche.  We are each a part of it.

Someday history will conclude, and we will see Him exactly as He is. At that time, God will separate the citizens of the Kingdom of Love from those of this world.  Those who chose to reflect the image of their selfish, wilderness god will be sealed in their decision to live away from Love forever.  Those who believe in God will celebrate together at the marriage supper of the Lamb.

After history will come eternity.  The creative force of His love will remake a new heaven and a new earth (Rev 21-22).  And there, those who believe in Love and have willingly responded to Love with love will spend the rest of forever knowing and being known; loving and being loved in return; serving each other in an everlasting kingdom of peace.  God in all of His glorious love will reign with His children acting as managers, governors, and presidents by His side for all eternity.  Creation will know Him in all the facets of His greatness.  It's what we've all been waiting for.

God is Love; He is full of extreme, visceral affection and compassion for all of creation, good and bad.  That changes everything.

> Rejoice in the Lord always.  I will say it again: Rejoice! Let your gentleness be evident to all. The Lord is near. Do not be anxious about anything, but in every situation, by prayer and petition, with thanksgiving, present your requests to God.  And the peace of God, which transcends all understanding, will guard your hearts and your minds in Christ Jesus.  (Phil 4:4-7, NIV)
>
> In this you rejoice, though now for a little while, if necessary, you have been grieved by various trials, so

that the tested genuineness of your faith—more precious than gold that perishes though it is tested by fire—may be found to result in praise and glory and honor at the revelation of Jesus Christ.  (1 Pet 1:6-7, ESV)

Consider it pure joy, my brothers and sisters, whenever you face trials of many kinds, because you know that the testing of your faith produces perseverance.  Let perseverance finish its work so that you may be mature and complete, not lacking anything.  (Jas 1:2-4, NIV)

Blessed is the man who remains steadfast under trial, for when he has stood the test he will receive the crown of life, which God has promised to those who love him. Let no one say when he is tempted, "I am being tempted by God," for God cannot be tempted with evil, and he himself tempts no one.  But each person is tempted when he is lured and enticed by his own desire.  Then desire when it has conceived gives birth to sin, and sin when it is fully grown brings forth death.

Do not be deceived, my beloved brothers.  Every good gift and every perfect gift is from above, coming down from the Father of lights, with whom there is no variation or shadow due to change.  (Jas 1:12-17, ESV)

Be patient, then, brothers and sisters, until the Lord's coming.  See how the farmer waits for the land to yield its valuable crop, patiently waiting for the autumn and spring rains.  You too, be patient and stand firm, because the Lord's coming is near… Brothers and sisters, as an example of patience in the face of suffering, take the prophets who spoke in the name of the Lord.  As you know, we count as blessed those who have persevered.  You have heard of Job's perseverance and have seen what the Lord finally brought about.  The Lord is full of compassion and mercy...

Is anyone among you in trouble? Let them pray.  Is anyone happy?  Let them sing songs of praise.  Is anyone among you sick? Let them call the elders of the church to pray over them and anoint them with oil in the name of the Lord.  And the prayer offered in faith will make the sick person well; the Lord will raise them up.  If they have sinned, they will be forgiven.  Therefore confess your sins to each other and pray for each other so that you may be healed.  The prayer of a righteous person is powerful and effective.

Elijah was a human being, even as we are. He prayed earnestly that it would not rain, and it did not rain on the land for three and a half years. Again he prayed, and the heavens gave rain, and the earth produced its crops.

My brothers and sisters, if one of you should wander from the truth and someone should bring that person back, remember this: Whoever turns a sinner from the error of their way will save them from death and cover over a multitude of sins.  (Jas 5:7-20, NIV)

"The thief comes only to steal and kill and destroy; I came that they may have life, and have it abundantly." (Jesus, John 10:10)

"I have told you these things, so that in me you may have peace.  In this world you will have trouble. But take heart!  I have overcome the world." (Jesus, John 16:33, NIV)

To contact the author with questions or comments:

waterfromwind@gmail.com

If you think this book could help someone else in their struggle, please take the time to encourage them with a review:

https://www.amazon.com/dp/B01LXC6QTF

or

https://amazon.com/review

Made in the USA
Las Vegas, NV
01 November 2023

80072341R00115